Texit.

The Hour of Our Disunion

Bruce McNabb &

Barbara Kennedy McNabb

ISBN: 978-1-966619-01-7

Contents

Dedication i

Acknowledgments iii

About the Authors v

Introduction 1

Chapter 1 5

Chapter 2 22

Chapter 3 55

Chapter 4 83

Chapter 5 110

Chapter 6 132

Chapter 7 151

Chapter 8 172

Chapter 9 209

Chapter 10 245

Chapter 11 252

Chapter 12 264

Acknowledgments

As a boy in Norman, Oklahoma, my mother allowed me to spend hours in the public library's children's section. The open invitation to become immersed in the written word was my life gift from Mom, who went to Glory in 2023. I will always treasure the passage to worlds known only to eyes that follow the lines in a book.

But chiefly, I am grateful to my loving bride Barbara. Without her gentle reassurance and encouragement, I never would have taken the step or stayed the course. I love you dearly, Barbara.

have usurped. It must be taken back. The constitution restored. Power is a zero-sum game. There is always a loser.

"When the Federal Republican Constitution of their country, which they swore to support, no longer has a substantial existence, and the whole nature of their government has been forcibly changed, without their consent, from a restricted federative republic, composed of sovereign states, to a consolidated central military despotism..."

Texas Declaration of Independence, March 2, 1836

Chapter 1

Boarding his Monday morning flight from Austin to Dulles, Charles "Charlie" O'Neal performed his usual three-meter scan to calm his mind of possible troublemakers. Spotting his seat and the decently attractive woman next to it, he stifled the small grin that gave away a welcomed first glance of approval. Within seconds of securing the seat belt, a soft, floral scent reached Charlie's nose, immediately causing uneasiness and unwanted distraction that he attempted to dismiss. How long had it been? Not Sophia's perfume, but nice, narcotic. Judas Priest, quit! Too much riding on this to be caught up with a girl. Sophia would kick him where it counts. Focus! Sophia would whisper, her nose barely touching his "better" ear, as she passed.

His final check of his phone raised the image of Sophia, his deceased wife. The loss always felt fresh. It was years ago when he believed he could manage and survive anything. Absolutely everything. Charlie glanced through emails and texts, applied the airplane mode, unfolded his tablet, and returned to his action items on second-level logistics, Casper team substitutes, and Gantt charts, swiftly knocking them out. He sensed other eyes. Unbelievable!

There is no privacy in all of hell's half-acre anymore. Slowly and deliberately, he turned to the next passenger, who couldn't seem to move her eyes away from his work.

"Can I help you?" Charlie demanded. Inhaling. Damn, she smelled good.

Tucking her chin, she said, "Sorry, sir, I couldn't help but…" Damn entitled strumpet.

"I'm Penny Townsend. I'm sorry, but are you planning a military thing? You look like a military guy."

O'Neal offered a slight smile, nodded negatively, and returned to his work. Get back to it—see the geofencing update on N. Tx Region, questions??— interval requirements changed? Mine III percenters, where are Independents on this? Texas Nationalist supporters on social media, funding sources, secure crowdfunding, technology requirements, "insurance" if the wheels come off? How do you insure an insurrection? Or a secession? Lloyds of London??

After the plane went wheels up, Charlie turned and asked, "And what do you do, Penny?"

"I'm the senior research analyst for Texas Policy Group, a boutique policy-writing firm in Austin. I'm sure you never heard of it."

He smiled. She was right. He'd never heard of it. "I hope you don't mind my asking, but who do you sell your assessments to?" asked Charlie.

Penny chuckled. "We 'sell' it to legislators, the governor, people like that mostly, decision-makers." Behind the veneer of the perfectly polite words and a new pair of Ray-Bans, Charlie was interested instantly. He touched his earlobe. More importantly, there may be some very enlightening intel to be gotten from resources occupying the seat on his right. She was in the game. What/who does she know? Ask questions. No wedding ring, simple and short hairstyle, a good set of wheels, it looks like. Get a legitimate reason to reconnect after the flight.

"What brings you to the swamp today, business or pleasure?" he asked.

"Obligation," answered Penny with a cute laugh. "Oh, it's business if those are the only choices."

Charlie nodded slightly, clearly not understanding. He smiled and returned to his work, knowing that less was more, at least for this exercise. Tapping out some requests for his advisors, Charlie needed no reminder that he hadn't filled in many of the "pieces" or smoothed over one or two oozing ulcers. Yep, he had to clean up some things, some relationships that would act as electrical conductors to send intel and energy where needed during this dangerous attempt leading up to eventual success as we faced the launch of a fledgling, but also free, republic lying next to the most powerful and angry nation in history. Notably, the "programmer slot" needs to be filled very soon. (Newly hatched vultures from MIT need not apply.) Someone who will converge the existing state systems and corresponding federal networks. Someone with vast connections in all the right agencies. As a giddy orchestral conductor, bringing new pieces of music to its musicians, O'Neal was tasked to... "Make it all work, Charlie, on day one, pal."

Until now, Texas was essentially spooning with The United States, and the clock was ticking. Meanwhile, Charlie and Penny chatted intermittently as they closed in on DC, and by the time the pilot chimed the final seat belt warning, they had agreed to have a drink at Penny's hotel, the Hamilton Hotel, which was less than half a mile from the White House at eighteen hundred hours. Upon arriving and cell phones ringing, collecting luggage, and figuring out the best way to get downtown during a busy morning, they waved to one another with see you laters and dove into their individual missions on point. Penny realized that she didn't bring anything that even alluded to feminine or soft. She had the Brooks and Burberry thing going on, nothing for this unexpected quick meeting with a perfect stranger in the hottest town. A drink date on Pennsylvania Avenue with a very mysterious, yet credible, and handsome NGO adrift in a swamp the size of the moon. The business suit, sans jacket, would have to do. To compensate, she quickly filled a tub and gave her legs a fresh shaving, hopped out, and lotioned all five-foot, ten inches of her female attributes, not all business. Her hair was always curly in DC. The humidity could choke you if you gave it an opportunity. Finally, she'd met a man with Charlie's genuineness and candor and big fat blue eyes. Not hard to look at.

Showered, shaved, and sparkling, she donned enticing sexless evening attire. She'd turn the blouse, and wear it backward. Why not? Live on the wild side. She needed to curb the sarcasm. He wasn't wearing a ring. Some men don't.

Her commitment to the foundation had cost her friendships, countless happy hours missed, required closely trimmed fingernails, an integral part of typing 120 words per minute, and hundreds of canceled gym workouts. She wondered how he felt about tattoos on women…

Down the street, still in the alphabet, not expecting the night to turn into anything, O'Neal hung his jacket in the hotel room closet, brushed his teeth, checked his phone and wallet, and left his hotel by way of the stairway and side door. Luckily, the weather favored his walk to the WMATA, the underground railway servicing the city. As he neared the Hamilton Hotel, he paused to look for any nefarious characters before entering.

The white marble tiled floor in the Hamilton reminded O'Neal of the Tremont in Galveston, a favorite of Sophia's, and where Charlie and Sophia discovered the pleasures of bathing in a big tub together. It seemed like everything reminded Charlie of Sophia. Damn the bunch of shitbirds that killed her.

The Hamilton lobby was sprinkled with people typical to all luxury hotels in DC, mostly European and Asian lobbyists and policy people. He navigated the edge of the lobby to the lounge, where he found Penny working a glass of red. From where he stood, Penny seemed to be in distant thought, staring at her small purse on the table. She could pass as an Eastern European operative. This would be fun.

"Good evening." Charlie checked his vintage wristwatch, bequeathed to him by Sophie's grandfather, who had been the Mayor of Naples for nearly two decades. "You are punctual, if not a bit early."

"Good evening to you," Penny answered. "I'm respectful of your time." She smiled; it was an inviting overture.

Two double Dewars later, two strangers on a plane were finding a good amount of common ground, especially in the political realm, both genuinely enjoying the others' humor, and O'Neal decided to slip in a meaningful question of Penny related to her relationship with the Texas Governor. "Tell me a little more about what you do for Texas Policy?"

Penny replied, "The Texas Policy Foundation? Well, most of my time is spent scouring government and other public news outlets, white papers, border-related articles, spying, listening to street chatter, and talking to the Hispanic Chambers of Commerce leadership. Also I co-chair the Governor's Council on Small Business." The cabernet had found its way to her brain and Penny experienced the euphoric stage associated with blood alcohol levels between 0.08 and 0.125. Excited and emboldened but still lucid.

Penny initiated her own plan of inquisition. "How often do you come to DC?"

"More often than I care to."

"Is there someone in particular here that you visit with?"

"Well, yes, congressional members from Texas, primarily." O'Neal then turned it around on Penny. "I suppose you and the governor have bounced around the pesky topic of the southern border?"

She rolled her eyes. "Once or twice." She sipped. "Why do you ask?"

"I'm curious about your firm's stance on the mess down there?" Charlie began, never taking his eyes off her mouth. He squeezed a fist behind his back to quell something bubbling inside.

"We have shared with the governor that the Chamber of Commerce policy position of 'maintaining the status quo on crossing restrictions,' according to our stats, poses a significant long-term risk to the state's autonomy and preservation of core values, among other things. He gets it. They all get it." Penny twisted slightly in her seat, showing a hint of unease and some thigh, which Charlie registered, and went back to watching her forming her words, sending him incendiary bytes through that fleshy portal, which separates information from propaganda, and takes acceptable faux words for white lies and deadly lies.

"I don't know." She sighed.

"Ok," said Penny. "Let's talk about something less official, like raw oysters on shaved ice?"

"Perfect," O'Neal said. His heart was racing. The waiter rushed over and returned, twirling a tray with two dozen pale pink oysters on pearly half shells. Penny flushed and looked down; Charlie laughed out loud. She was fun. Unabashedly. The wine was her favorite, a French Burgundy. It warmed her. She was staring at his mouth as he spoke. He touched her hand.

She said, "I am sorry about my nosiness on the plane earlier, and you didn't answer my question. Are you working on a military plan? Is it something classified? You seemed so intense."

"That's several questions all at once, you know. First, no, I'm not exactly working on a military plan, or op. And it's not classified, but it is sensitive. My seriousness? That's just habit, getting centered, being focused. Distractions know how to find me."

"So, what is it that you do?" she asked.

"I'm Chief Risk Officer for NRG Energy. We operate a nuclear power facility in south Texas and some related operations. Mostly fairly mundane stuff, but my group is responsible for anticipating and preventing less-than-desirable events that might occur."

"Were you in the military?"

"Yep, a long time ago. What does the governor really want our border situation to look like?"

She smiled. "To tell the truth," she offered, "he's a chameleon and he'll probably pull off whatever he's cooking up. It annoys me, but he's got the big office on Congress Avenue. I don't. I won't ask if you have business with him. It's no secret he is a purely political beast. He is the governor and all, and he is very important for my career since he's asked me to directly provide more and more data and then placed me on the council. He's been very clear to me that I report directly to him, not to his staff, but to him. He's just slimy, and everyone that works with him knows he's a selfish ass-kissing narcissist."

"Perfect for a governor, huh?" Charlie smiled. Sarcasm was a bad habit he'd picked up in his travels.

The disappearance of the oysters was followed by beautifully presented beef tenderloin medallions resting in au jus, cradled by steamed broccolini. Penny began noticing details of O'Neal, the scarred hands, a hint of nervousness, and occasionally scanning the room, only to rejoin the conversation without missing a syllable.

Almost as if he was expecting trouble… Penny, in fact, proved to be quite articulate and well-informed, yet able and willing to intertwine humor into several topics of conversation. Charlie found himself smitten and freshly alive for the first time since Sophia's passing years ago. Penny seemed equally enchanted by O'Neal's direct but boyish nature. Suddenly, he was self-conscious of his posture, his grooming, and even his word selection. Another two hours disappeared, and Charlie needed to find the loo. "Would you please excuse me? I need to powder my nose."

A chuckle and smirk offered Penny's approval and Charlie stood, scanned the room, and strode toward the restrooms, baring his limp only slightly. Penny watched and wondered what would cause an otherwise good specimen of a man to have a limp.

She would later reflect that the moment was a Rubicon crossing. Another glass of Burgundy later, Penny realized that Charlie had not reappeared, so she got up from her seat and marched to the restrooms, first men's, where she caught the maître di finishing his business. She apologized but searched the men's room in a manner to make Dick Tracy proud before doing the same in the ladies' room. The waiting staff all shrugged: crazy Americans.

"He's gone…gone gone." Dammit, girl. I thought he'd at least have the balls to say he had had enough… and he'd even walked the check.

The next day, a screeching hotel alarm clock jolted Penny from her hard-fought sleep and her mind swirled in its second dance with the Burgundy from the night past. She gradually gained her wits, and she turned over and revisited the night with O'Neal. Did she say something to run him off? It didn't make sense. Weren't they both enjoying themselves? He was the first guy in years that had something going on for himself. Was he acting? Pretending that he was having a good time? She saw him looking around. Was it for a quick exit? He acted like he was having a really good time. Ugh, her head hurt. How was your date, Penny? Date? What date? It was awful. She was pretty sure she embarrassed herself.

Flipping open her laptop, Penny watched a swallow outside her window dart about and finally light on the sill corner. As her laptop chimed its readiness, Penny began to search for more information on O'Neal, finding a few articles noting his promotion at NRG Energy, pausing to zoom in on the photo of Charlie being congratulated by Michael Darst. Retired Army Ranger, A&M graduate. No mention of family. Lived near Victoria. It didn't make sense. She checked the time, rushed into her skirt, dropped her hairbrush two or three times, and flagged a cab to the Rayburn Building, hardly giving her enough time to clear her hangover from her head. A quick review of her notes reminded her of the details around the inconsistencies of the committee report on NGO funding in Texas, and she scribbled a few comments for her to cover while with Congresswoman Mays.

Penny swallowed hard as she began her walk to Rayburn. She disliked Ms. Mays to her very core, yet she knew that Mays wasn't smart by any measure, and she would need to only find a crack in the congresswoman's story to know where next to go for more information. Mays would never meet with her without a senior staffer, and this meeting would likely be her last civil conversation with Mays, if there was one at all. Just as Penny expected, Penny's friend Amanda, who was chief of staff for the congresswoman, greeted Penny and asked that she find a seat at the small table as both awaited the legislator to make her grand entry. It didn't take long.

After a perfectly scripted welcome, Mays began her stare into Penny's eyes, leaned forward to get her elbows on the table, and said, "Let's cut to the chase, what do you say, Missy? Your firm has been less than favorable regarding my work here in Congress and it has made for some uncomfortable meetings with the Texas Caucus. Of course, most of the folks are just rich white guys that have the stick. But you know that, right? So, what exactly, I mean exactly, can I do for you?" There it was, that small trigger showing her lack of confidence.

"Penny, the congresswoman is really short on time today. Could you please tell us?" prodded faithful Amanda.

"Of course, I'd hate to hold up the congresswoman. I suppose it would be very helpful, Congresswoman Mays, if you would shed some light for me on the relatively large discrepancies of the committee's report on the funding of NGO Our Lady of Perpetual Light, as opposed to the Budget Office report."

"This is such a waste of my time," quipped the congresswoman as she stood, wheeled, and re-entered her private office.

"Well," said Penny, "that didn't take much of her time, did it?"

Amanda appeared genuinely embarrassed and began divulging exceedingly, almost to the point Penny couldn't hold any more in her head. The tiny spiral notebook that she pulled from her bag was brought ready and she furiously began recording the salient points of the staffer.

"Just so that I'm clear," Penny stated, "is it your understanding, Amanda, that the two-million-dollar surplus between the reports is almost entirely due to minimal and anonymous contributions?" Looking across the room, the chief of staff quietly sighed and responded, "That is correct… I'm sorry but I need to show you out now."

Back in the hallway, Penny grabbed her phone, checked her email, and shot a quick text to her boss at the foundation. "Two million dollars plus at Our Lady confirmed. I'll be in touch. Later."

Meanwhile, by the time Charlie could look around with any ability to discern his surroundings through the duct tape covering his eyes, the DC sun had begun its march westward over the Potomac

River. From his vantage point of being taped to the carpet, he surmised that he was in a cheap hotel somewhere. Craning his neck to the left and ripping hair from his scalp, he caught a glimpse of a television with Oprah baiting her audience of extras. He struggled unsuccessfully and instantly saw a man leering over him, complete with latex gloves, a ski mask, and something small in the man's hand which was jammed into O'Neal's face. Instinctively, O'Neil recoiled, fearing a stun gun, but instead it only emitted the click of a button. "Mr. O'Neal, please save your energy and remain calm and quiet. The man holding this recorder has authority to use every means necessary to detain you. You will be released soon, assuming you act accordingly. Thank you in advance for your cooperation."

Charlie tried to relax, with his mind racing for answers. Has to be political, but who? A mainstream Republican? Anarchist Dem? What is that congresswoman's name from East Houston? The Marxist lady. He patted his face; what drug did that guy use on me? Several hours passed before Charlie once again awoke, and he began frantically wrestling to get free from the duct tape handcuffs digging into his wrists more intensely with every attempt. The door opened and O'Neal watched a small silhouette enter after passing car headlights, and a voice authoritatively instructed the kidnapper to leave the room for a few minutes. In just seconds, Charlie was alone with the darkly clad figure.

"I hope that, in spite of the current arrangements, you are well and unharmed, Mr. O'Neal. It is imperative that your team doesn't hear from you for a few days, which will be more than enough time." Charlie muffled a comment behind the duct tape and the man chuckled and peeled the tape from Charlie's mouth.

"You were saying…"

Charlie gathered his thoughts and calmly said, "You don't really know me, because if you did, I'd be dead. What do you need time for?"

He smiled, slightly turned his face away and said, "We have learned an impressive amount regarding your team over the last few days, and I must admit, your little group has done quite a lot given your lack of resources. Your stay with us and some secondary communications will convince your people that you've reached a point where you can't follow through and are disappearing yourself, a Clinton era term, of course." O'Neal was taped silent, but underneath the duct tape he was the one smiling.

The hotel room soon held three additional goons to ensure his transition to the awaiting van outside would go off without a hitch.

The next injection Chalie received took him into a deep and chaotic sleep. Dreams of Sophia's final hours in the hospital ICU where she repeatedly apologized for taking the COVID vaccine, both, and a booster as he had pleaded. She'd betrayed him in the worst way. Rushing back with all reality came the annoying sounds of the medical monitoring, the pale eyes of his dead bride who suddenly died from blood clots appearing without a definitive source or injury, "cause unknown." Her once golden Mediterranean skin was pale, her eyes reflecting extreme anguish. Fear. Regret. Instantly triggered, the entire scene was replaced by the deafening gunfight in Afghanistan with the same chaos, yelling, inciting, same rounds whizzing, and chunks of adobe flying everywhere.

When O'Neal regained consciousness, he intuitively remained still, slowly cracking an eye open and taking into account everything he could register. After some time, he was able to quietly reach a kneeling posture, and he strained his eyes to make sense of the almost total darkness. There appeared to be a single door whose threshold allowed a tiny sliver of light to sneak into the room from the outside. He quickly knew that he had been left alone, and the duct tape restraining him was effortlessly cut by the edge of the table legs close by. Square breathe…

The door was locked, and he rapidly ran his hands over the door's frame and hinges, finding a two-key deadbolt lock above the handle. The doors hinges, however, were on the inside and O'Neal grinned for the first time since he was taken from the restaurant. In a perfectly efficient manner, the table's edge was cornered under the head of the door hinge pin and O'Neal put his shoulder into levering the table enough to pop the top pin completely free. The lower hinge proved much more of a challenge, but a table leg, broken off, proved to be effective in prying up the pin. Holding the table leg, he listened for anyone nearby, and hearing none, he pried the door off and slowly opened it into the room. Across the hallway was a glass-walled area complete with soft drink machines, a snack dispenser, a small conference table and a television on the wall directly across from Charlie.

The goon who had earlier stood over Charlie in the hotel room was stuffing his pie hole, glued to the television. Slowly dropping low, he checked himself and the table leg, checked both directions down the hall, then eased out of the doorway, replacing the door on its hinges and he slithered about fifty feet before getting to his feet and finding an unobserved pedestrian door at the end of the hallway. Once outside, O'Neal again quickly scanned the area, rolled up the door mat and ran for the fence appearing closest to a wooded area. The mat served its purpose well, blunting the razor wire enough for O'Neal to overcome it with only minor cuts to show for it. The thick undergrowth swallowed him, and the yells of frustrated security personnel gradually faded as he made his way through the dense network of vines and shrubs below the hardwood canopy.

"It is the unemotional, reserved, calm, detached warrior who wins." - Sun Tzu

Chapter 2

O'Neal's upbringing was not unlike the millions of post-Viet Nam era children in the U.S. His father grew up in rural Arkansas as the eighth of ten children to an unlicensed chiropractor who deserted the family after the last child was born. O'Neal's father was as serious as it got, and he accepted an early high school graduation and enlisted in the 4th Division, United States Marine Corp, in time to participate in fighting Japanese on the Mariana Islands. Upon his return home in 1945, the man, handsome and fit, became a football star at the University of Texas and subsequently coached at the high school and collegiate level before journeying through several industries, always leaning on the past glory of his playing days.

Charlie grew up in the shadow of his father and brought upon himself immense pressure to prove his worth to his father. Charlie incurred several substantial injuries along the way, some properly treated and some hidden, which would later serve him in managing setbacks. O'Neal did not look forward to leaving the dugout after a baseball game or leaving the field after a football game where his father often met him with a critically harsh review of his performance.

Like the many who followed the unraveling of the war in Vietnam, which encouraged a growing mistrust for all representatives, senators, lobbyists, and the donor class, Charlie joined the army only to repay his stack of student loans for the pleasure of four years at Texas A&M University in the face of an economic recession. Were it not for the prank Charlie led, which resulted in the power loss across town from the tunnels under campus, O'Neal would have skated through to an engineering degree unblemished. Albeit distasteful, the army afforded ample opportunity in an era when the military lacked both respect and recruits less than a generation after the broad-scale slaughter of America's finest in southeast Asia.

Both physically and emotionally strong, Charlie signed a contract and breezed through basic, officer candidate school, Airborne training, Ranger assessment and selection program, psyops, and was assigned to 75th Ranger Regiment, Ft. Moore, Georgia.

The accomplishments of 75th Ranger Regiment are legendary and quietly recorded as are other special operations groups. In Afghanistan, a platoon-sized Ranger security element conducted multiple missions in the early 2000s. In June 2005, members of RRD Team 3 were tasked to help recover the bodies of the United

States Navy SEALS killed during Operation Red Wings. During this operation, the team was responsible for hunting down and killing the remaining insurgents who had engaged the SEALS. The team members followed the blood trails and tracked the insurgents to their hiding places and killed them. Once engaged, Team 3 was also responsible for killing the re-enforcements that came to the aid of the Taliban fighters. The Regimental Reconnaissance Company (formerly known as Regimental Reconnaissance Detachment, or RRD) is an elite special operations force believed to have become part of JSOC later in 2005 due to its extensive training and unique capabilities to conduct special reconnaissance and close target reconnaissance (CTR) operations, and advanced force operations (AFO).

Charlie met Sophia at Martin Army Community Hospital, Ft. Moore, when O'Neal tore a bicep during training. As Charlie was anesthetized, Sophia conspired with the surgical team to apply several temporary tattoos on O'Neal with colorful sharpies, so that upon his exiting the emergency surgery he was unknowingly a walking billboard of peace signs, "peace not war" and flower child daisy chains. The recovery room was all laughter until Charlie saw the drawings, threw off his robe and proceeded to float down the hallway singing the sixties classic, "If you're going to San Francisco…"

The surgical nurse coordinator turned to Sophia, thrusting Charlie's gown into her arms and said, "It's the anesthesia… makes them…what's the word? Oh, yes, randy. That is, indecent exposure. Well, better get after him." She waved Sophie down the hall, "Before someone does call nine one one."

Sophia caught up with O'Neal and wrapped him in his hospital gown. The whole surgical ward enjoyed the show. Charlie spun around to Sophia to thank her. Her deep caramel eyes. Her lips. The way she smelled. They were something to behold. Indeed.

Sophia, first-generation Italian-American, a product of Athens, Georgia, teemed with enthusiasm for emergency medicine and quick, mostly positive, outcomes they generated. Big highs. Big sighs. And with their matched risk tolerance and stomach for it—what could possibly go wrong? Soon, they became a couple to be reckoned with. Her passionate manners and eye for art and style complemented Charlie's steady square corners and predictable mannerisms, as flashy as any feasibility study. It worked. Yin-and-Yang. When he was with her, everything hummed. The bloody size of a cannon ball this.

Sophia's mother Victoria and father Giuseppe found their way to Athens, where Giuseppe taught at the University of Georgia. Giuseppe, an industrial engineering graduate of The Milano Leonardo campus of the Polytechnic University in Milan, Italy, was recruited by the University of Georgia, a three-hour drive to Ft. Moore.

Thoughts of Sophia consumed Charlie most days, all day. A curandera, Sophia stepped into Charlie's life and raised him up notch-by-notch into a state of supreme health. Hours would simply vanish as they dove into conversations of philosophy, divinity, and books. Prescriptive meds for pain and other ailments were flushed and were replaced with whole foods and organic supplements. Vitamins and herbs, oils and flower petals. Garlic, in absolutely everything. Everywhere. Nothing changes if nothing changes. These changes, gradual yet discernable, gave Charlie reason to want more, to do more. To be more. This was not synergy. It was divine. It was in the first two months of their romance when Sophia drew the line with Charlie and called him out on his drinking, effectively allowing him to choose her, or the bottle.

He would remember always the exact spot where he was when, over the phone, Sophia said, "I'm not having anything to do with a man who can't speak in clear, cogent sentences. Last night, you made no sense, and I could tell you had been drinking. I'm not telling you what to do, but if you want to drink, you'll need to do that with someone else." It took O'Neal less than five seconds to respond.

"That's easy," he said. "I choose you."

In that moment, decades of drinking as far back as high school vanished. Alcohol recidivism, according to some data, has a rate north of eighty percent. Charlie's relationship with alcohol was that of a mistress, quick to fill the hole that lost love, or requited love, leaves behind. And there was no question, Sophia more than filled the canyon inside Charlie. He could not believe his amazing fortune. It humbled him, which allowed him the honor of being prompted and able to look around corners, and to know what's coming. To love and protect… This is how we joined and lived as one.

Until she died. The life Sophia gave him. Man, she knew things. Things that were happening around her. And around the world. Things discerned by nobody else. God spoke to her, and she listened. She saw it. She played hunches. Then, she researched it until she had scientific validation gleaned from tomes of peer reviews. And then she would or would not place her bet. When she lovingly admonished you for betting against her about who would become the next speaker of the house, she won that bet and O'Neal got mad. Wait. What?

She said, "Charlie, don't bet against me. When I tell you to hit the deck, the next thing and only thing I want to hear next is the sound of your body hitting the ground. Because while you're busy asking twenty questions and betting against me, a rocket just came through the wall and blew out the house."

"Damn," he said. "Do you know how to use a gun?"

"Yes."

"Damn," he said, and he smiled that 'I got all six numbers smile.' Bingo.

For Charlie, it was safe once again, being with someone who knew of his down days, knew of the unspoken challenges, and who was a committed partner who felt his heart beating a mile away. He couldn't hide anything from her because she just knew. In a matter of weeks, he began to know a bit of her feelings as well and occasionally he would make a comment to her that was, in fact, telepathic. I was thinking about my new Italian friend, Mr. Gelato. I looked up at Sophia, and she said, "Whose car are we taking?"

Sophia was both complex and fragile, like a hummingbird that can't be mishandled. Early on, Charlie might have innocently approached Sophia from behind and startled her enough to put her off for the rest of the day. Was she kidding? He watched her and it really was involuntary, triggered by loud and sudden noises, especially behind her. Him coming in through the back door. Mild PTSD. So, Charlie learned to announce himself upon entering their home or bedroom just to prevent startling her, as someone would announce himself to prevent a gun being pointed at an intruder. He vowed to bring her strong faith in life everlasting, and flowers just because.

In the meantime, she was safe so she could remain in a positively charged stratum. She was musing, she teased, about writing a book. He told her he thought it was a great idea.

In the months to follow, weight loss, increased sleep, and a mind clearer than in years prior were manifestations of an ill patient making a connection with a healer. The two souls twisted together in a manner known only to those that had traveled together for many years. Charlie's military status would soon be sending him to areas of intense conflict and violence, and yet together they plotted a future together someplace. Sophia soon realized that Charlie was manifested by her conversations with God. He was her "twin flame" she said dreamily, and she had every intention of traveling the rest of her life on Earth with him. She believed that God would bring them home together and that she would not be disappointed when He did.

A slight, bearded cowboy boot-wearing justice of the peace joined Sophia and Charlie in matrimony, where Sophia donned a shimmering dusty-gold dress. The essence of time prevented a traditional church wedding, and they would later reflect that they did indeed feel God's presence in the modest metal county building where the ceremony was held. Several "firsts" found their way into Sophia and Charlie's life. Flickering and jeweled, a tiara held her raven hair from her face. She was as beautiful as any goddess. Their bathtub was larger than some, but not much. Vintage rock and roll and a few candles provided the backdrop for long soakings and deep conversations, four legs intertwined with knees poking up out of the water like Loch Nessie.

Raising children and sandy beaches were big items of discussion in the tub, and it was there that Sophia was able to safely reveal her closest-held demons to Charlie until the water grew cool enough to pull the stopper and bring more hot water. As she rose from the tub, the shimmer of her beautiful form in the candlelight caused Charlie to be mesmerized, unable to speak or even move. He would often reflect later on her perfectly formed breasts and ultra feminine and graceful movements. Later, after soaking, he watched her sleep, and he thanked God for her.

His army years hardened and matured him. The bad things required to be done by good men like Charlie drove him to his knees daily in the early morning darkness. The habit of prayer allowed him to lay off all the guilt borne by his actions during confrontations with the enemy. "Operation Enduring Freedom," the official label of the war in Afghanistan beginning in 2001, presented O'Neal several opportunities to demonstrate his ability to operate in dire circumstances. Operation Rhino was a raid led by the United States Army's 75th Ranger Regiment (Regimental Reconnaissance Company) and (3rd Ranger Battalion).

On the night of 19 October 2001, before the Rangers dropped, several targets on and around the objective were targeted by U.S. air power, first by bombs dropped from B-2 stealth bombers, then from orbiting AC-130 aircraft. Following the air strikes, the four MC-130 Combat Talon aircraft flew over the drop zone (DZ) at 800 feet. In zero illumination, the Rangers proceeded to exit the MC-130s. O'Neal's company of rangers, accompanied by a sniper team, secured the area and established strategic positions to defend against potential counterattacks.

The compound was completely empty and the presence of combat cameramen and a Navy P-3C Orion command-and-control plane overhead highlighted the importance placed on capturing propaganda footage during the operation. No U.S. casualties were suffered in the operation itself, but two Rangers assigned to a combat search and rescue element supporting the mission were killed when their MH-60L helicopter crashed at Objective Honda in Pakistan—a temporary staging site used by a company of Rangers from 3/75. The helicopter crashed due to a brownout. The entire mission, which claimed two of O'Neal's brothers, was nothing more than a publicity stunt for the Pentagon. Charlie knew it.

Endless things to be grateful for, earnest pleas for forgiveness, requests for guidance, all among the tenants of his prayers to God, and through one hundred plus days in country, one example after another proved his deep-rooted understanding that God had a plan for him.

O'Neal had grown numb. Soon enough, compartmentalized. Sophie suggested that he might feel better talking about it. He wouldn't. He could never imagine telling it to anyone. But, when he remembered why he was there, when he encountered the local kids playing kick-the-coconut in the dirt road, barefoot, the steely Ranger went as butter in a hot pan.

It was during one of the many night operations that O'Neal suffered a career-ending injury. While clearing a room in a tiny Afghan village, O'Neal's team was met with an overwhelming Taliban element and in what was a typically chaotic gunfight, rounds from a Taliban AK found their way into Charlie's upper thigh, severing an artery and shattering his femur. Massively losing blood pressure, O'Neal was saved by a teammate with a tourniquet and dragging him out of range, to a safe area. Several surgical procedures were necessary for O'Neal to regain his usual mobility and gait, and sympathetic regimental leadership directed that his recovery be undertaken at the center for the Intrepid in San Antonio, until he was ready to run marathons. It was only a short two-hour drive for Sophia.

Charlie had a foot out of the door with the military, heading for private industry after Afghanistan, when he received the offer by the DIA. The US Army was insistent that Charlie acquire the skills required to become an impressive possessor of the most technical requirements regarding power systems disruption and geofencing, the use of GPS or RFID technology to create a virtual geographic boundary, enabling software to trigger a response when a mobile device enters or leaves a particular area. DIA expanded O'Neal's capabilities and network, but he quickly stepped away from the government when the opportunity presented itself to go to private industry in Southeast Texas.

Sophia worked for a regional hospital system in south Texas that operated two major hospital facilities in Victoria and several satellite care facilities in towns like Rockport, Cuero, Hallettsville, Yoakum, Goliad, and Edna.

As COVID-19 spread through the area in 2019, protocols for healthcare workers and first responders changed weekly, mayors and governors and statesmen, no one could keep up, like the *Wheel of Fortune* spin. Always wear a mask, wear two masks, wear hazmat suits, hazmat suits not required, and on it went. Vaccinations became mandatory as they became readily available in early 2021. There were drive-up swabbing kiosks in shopping centers and midtowns—in any town. For Sophia and her co-workers, the first twelve months of the pandemic were no more than a normal seasonal flu. Turn-out in those cases were sporadic, most treatment was quick, and seldom were patients re-admitted.

"There's no such thing as a warp-speed vaccine." They knew it was, in fact, the most dangerous and most damaging drug in the history of medicine, and the government, induced by big pharma, convinced the medical community that it was safe, necessary, and very effective. As if the medical industry needed any additional rationale, payouts to providers were multiplied if COVID was identified as the cause of death attributed to the patient treatment. Hospital groups and their boards were effectively mandated to follow CDC-developed protocols regarding vaccinations and patient treatment policies or face government funding interruptions, and untenured staff reduced. People were being arrested for wanting to be left alone and fired for refusing the vaccine.

Illusionary vaccine syringe props found their way into C-level personnel who gladly and very publicly received "the injection." The jab was mandated and the un-vaxed traitors got to sit in the corner and face the wall. Personnel at The Centers for Disease Control did not require their own to become vaccinated, and privately, Ivermectin was doled out for prophylactic administration. Questioning compliance threatened careers of the country's most vital segment of healthcare providers, law enforcement, and first responders, as well as America's military. All the while, the outspoken advocates for the country's vaccination efforts never intended on personally receiving an untested genetically altering injection themselves. Hollywood and snake oil changed everything. And those who did not offer up the arm as human sacrifice were ostracized as murderers and conspirators. Meanwhile, hamsters were dropping dead on the wheel.

Once the various COVID vaccines were commonly available and the public broadly received them, the experiences in emergency rooms changed markedly. Everyone knew the rules. Big pharma and the medical elite grew ever more voracious, and swindled their patients, each and every one of them, that they swore to heal. The volume of patients climbed dramatically and patients who had received the vaccine were sicker than the "pure bloods," required more resources, and tended to become the hospital admissions. Although treatment protocols continued to shift through the pandemic, more and more patients died in hospitals on the ventilators.

Sophia's professional life required much of her, and she felt very much her candle had wicks burning at both ends. She thus far refused the vaccine, with Charlie's total support for her defending her right to protect her own body. But, ended up taking a religious exemption for now. One indelible brick at a time.

As COVID-19 changed the world and as bureaucrats of all stripes grew incrementally more tyrannical with their employees on vaccination, Sophia became convinced that the vaccine played a major part in the caseload spiral of COVID patients and the similar spiral of related deaths.

Then there was a shortage. Millions of masks disappeared. Imagine a Saturday morning cartoon. Then the tests, endless tests. Until finally the test comes back positive. Then graphene hydroxide is discovered in a testing cotton swab and patients are dying of strokes. Children. Then ear strokes causing sudden hearing loss, permanent. People are dropping dead. Now it's the "jab."

As cases of COVID flooded her hospital, Sophia's position required her to lead a team assigned to older patients experiencing severe symptoms requiring additional attention. She watched patients deteriorate when ventilation was initiated and over the coming weeks gained consensus with her colleagues that clearly pointed to a deliberate plan to remove patients from the system one big bite at a time, obtaining federal funds at an increased rate, and replace the patient to replay the trick by increasing the patient turnover. Sophia found her way to the hospital and her closest colleagues began to privately discuss the massive corruption and agreed to gather proof to bring a halt to the large and widespread kill. Sophia frequented the hospital morgue, and a confidant there shared with her a smoking gun—the blood clots recovered only from the vaccinated victims.

"Sorry to bother you, Carol," said Sophia, "but please tell me more about what you're seeing."

"I'm sworn to secrecy, Sophia. You know I'll get fired if they find out!" blurted Carol, the forensic pathologist. "This is crazy!"

"Carol, please, believe that I will not breathe a word to another living soul. But I do have to tell Charlie. But no one else. I promise," Sophia reassured. "What are you seeing?"

"It's horrific what they have done. And you know if it's happening here, it's happening elsewhere. The stakes are too high to dismiss this. What are we going to do?"

Carol paused, sighed, she continued, "I have noted this in my reports, Sophia, but the majority of COVID-related deaths show extraordinary arterial thrombosis, and the clotting is inside and bleeding, clotting endlessly until, what? The heart bleeds out, the brain? But…"

"It's very unusual. Something is causing massive hemorrhaging but…" Carol stared at the specimen container. "Here is what I think. This little vax is a killing machine." Sophia gasped. "What's wrong? Are you okay, Sophia?"

"Nothing, nothing, please go on." Sophia sat down. The room began to spin.

"Well," Carol spoke in a low voice, "it's a finger-print-less murder."

"What? What does that mean?

"A million little cuts. Something is cutting the veins and the arteries, slowly… it isn't one long clot I am seeing. It's a hundred little clots stuck together."

Sophia gave Carol a quick hug, looked her in the eyes and said, "Don't worry, Carol. This will stay between you and me. Can I tell you something? You know they have me up on floor four with the geriatric cases? These people are being killed, Carol, suffocated. The ventilation protocol is causing pulmonary embolism. I'm certain something really, really awful is happening here. Please be careful."

"Hey, Sophia, aren't you glad you held your ground? Resisted the JAB? Atta girl."

Sophia waved goodbye, turned the corner, and heaved lunch.

She found her way back to her section of the hospital, but her mind was swimming with possibilities. That night, as she nursed a joint of cannabis on the back porch, Charlie watched her from the door, concerned about her fidgeting. She studied the lit end of the cigarette, softly turning it against the ash tray while almost muttering to herself about the discovery she'd made earlier in the day. Her toes, painted a faint color of champaign, curled over the rail of the porch, and she slowly rocked the patio chair as she silently deliberated.

"Sophia, what?" Charlie inquired as he walked out onto the porch.

Looking up, tears streamed down Sophia's cheeks and she wiped them with the back of her hands. Visibly shaken, Charlie came to her side and placed his hand on her shoulder. They looked at each other and several minutes passed before Sophia could speak.

“They are purposely killing people, Charlie,” she murmured. “Old people.”

“Who are killing people?” Charlie leaned into her.

“The hospital, the government, nursing homes.” She shrugged. “They’re killing COVID patients, and a lot of them. The protocols are pushing the patients off the cliff.” Sophia took a deep breath and steadied herself. “For some reason, the autopsies are showing massive blood clots; it’s all so scary and nobody but Carol is questioning any of it. Do you think our government would do that?” she whispered, not to be overheard.

O’Neal tried to console Sophia and searched for his words, knowing first-hand the dark capabilities of the regime.

“Who have you spoken to about this, Sophia?” he asked.

“Just two colleagues in the hospital. They see it also,” she told him.

“Please listen to me.” Charlie firmly grabbed her shoulder until she looked up at him. “I understand that you feel the need to do what is right, but you must be very careful with all this. The hospital is a corporation, and corporations are soulless creatures. They will do whatever is needed to suppress this and it will be bad for your health, do you understand me? People have been killed for much less.”

He kneeled next to Sophia, wrapped his arms around her, and she exploded in tears and uncontrolled anguish. His heart sank with the knowledge that the government would not allow this discovery to go any further. It was only a matter of time. The evening turned into darkness and the calls of the mourning doves gave way to the night shift of cicadas who seamlessly assumed the role of background music for the O'Neals who remained entwined until early morning.

Still dark, O'Neal poured his first cup and settled into his favorite red leather chair by the fireplace, embracing the quiet darkness and bringing his entire life into pinpoint focus. He flipped through the headlines on his phone, then opened his daily readings of Psalms, Old Testament lore, and Gospel texts. This was his favorite time of day, when it was still dark and still quiet. He carefully got to his knees in the stillness of the early morning.

So much to thank you for, O Lord…

Getting back on his feet was not as simple as before the war and yet he would never mutter a complaint to anyone about it, ever.

Texting, he said, "Mr. Darst, this is Charlie O'Neal. I need to talk to you, and I'm afraid we need to speak in person."

"Is everything all right?" responded Darst.

"Can we meet at the park today? Say, noon. I'll bring some lunch. White or rye?"

"Sure, ok, Charlie. Is there something I need to know right away?" Darst asked.

"It's not like that. I can fill you in there."

"I'll take Sue's dog for a walk. Oh, and Charlie, just so we never have to have this conversation ever again, I like bologna on Wonder bread with mayo."

Charlie didn't know what he'd say. Or what he wanted or needed from Michael.

Charlie kissed Sophia goodbye and placed a cup of coffee, mostly milk, on her nightstand. Walking out he stopped to pet his retriever, Jolie, saying, "Guard the house and Sophia, good girl."

O'Neal lost all track of all time heading up highway 59 to Houston, Charlie didn't know what he'd say.

After crossing the outer loop, he regained his senses and smiled when he considered how fortunate he was to have a boss who really understood the dangerous decline of this monumentally global invasion occurring in the United States. It was a hijack, clear and simple. Even the good guys had sold out to grand larceny and debauchery. (They were shorting the dollar and laundering it to Pandora papers.) Texas was ready to secede.

As Charlie approached the park, he searched for any indication of a problem, spotting Darst at a bench, legs crossed casually and as he approached, noticed Darst studying a pigeon serenading him with dance. He rose to meet Charlie, shaking his hand and showing him to sit next to him. O'Neal felt a wave of relief as he sat down.

Interesting, he thought, that this one man brought him some peace of mind. Charlie extended the sandwich bag to Darst who smiled a quick smile.

"Ok, Charlie, it's just us and you have my undivided attention. What can I do to lighten your obvious burden?"

O'Neal breathed in deeply, paused, and then said "It's my wife, Sophia, who's gotten herself into a really bad situation, I'm afraid. I'm sorry to take you out of the office for personal business, but I just need to share some things with you and get your advice."

Darst pushed his sunglasses up but didn't say a word. He clasped his hands in his lap and half smiled at Charlie. Then nodded.

Charlie continued, "You may recall that she's a lead nurse at the hospital in Victoria. She's in the ER, surrounded by newborns, and happy as a lark. She's talking about seeding the garden and what do I think? Well, frankly, I think she already is—just a little husbandry observation. I don't even think she realizes it, she's that busy at work, putting in fourteen hours, wearing a mask all day. Seeing patient after patient, exposed to the worst. Now, they're wearing hazmat suits. We decided not to take any vaccines at this time.

"All that said, she's observing patients who were ready to discharge dying of heart attacks and patients forced onto respirators only to smother and die. The hospital's protocols appear to be centered around increasing the velocity of patient turnover, and I don't mean in a good way. The death count is increasing very rapidly, retirement community vans are working three shifts, and some strange things have been discovered in the morgue during necropsy. Sophia has been discussing the situation with a couple of her colleagues and they're all scared."

Darst lifted his chin, slightly turned his head away and said, "And you think there is something going on there, don't you?"

"Yessir," O'Neal said. "Sophia knows what she's talking about. There is no winter flu this year, miraculously? And this is not a vaccine, says Sophia. I agree. If the government catches wind of this, they will all be in danger."

Darst raised his hand to stop O'Neal from continuing. "Say no more, at least for the time being. Where is Sophia now?"

"At work, until eighteen hundred hours at least," O'Neal replied.

"Alright then, Charlie, here's what we'll do for starters. Let's get Demi Riojas from Cuero involved. Do you know him?"

"Yes, sir, I've met him."

"Then you probably know he's good-to-go. Fifth group, Eighteen Bravo."

"Yes, sir. You mean to put him on me?" O'Neal asked.

"Yes, he'll be all yours for the time being. This smells very bad…I'll get him up to speed and he'll drop you a pin of his whereabouts, probably out on the highway outside of town if I had to guess. He will have gear for both of you, including burner phones. Continue to use your phone as if nothing has changed, ok? Send me a text from your burner phone asking me if I found your dog. You need to get to the hospital when her shift is over and be aware of their overhead cameras, ok, and make sure they record y'all leaving together, and tell her you're taking her out to dinner. And make sure she tells her accomplices. Demi will be the eyes and ears you need to get through the next few days, but Charlie, hear me out on this… it will go badly for Sophia and her compatriots if the Gs hear about this. You should prepare yourself for the worst-case scenario. Just know that I got your six and a real price will be exacted on these government pricks. I have about had enough. You've got a week or so but get going."

"The art of war teaches us to rely not on the likelihood of the enemy's not coming, but on our own readiness to receive him." — Sun Tzu

By Feb. 23, 1991, the 1st Marine Expeditionary Force was controlling two reinforced Marine Divisions poised to strike Iraqi forces. In the lead up to the invasion, the Marines worked furiously to find gaps in the minefield that they could strike through. They also frequently clashed with Iraqi forces when conducting artillery raids and during the pre-emptive Battle of Khafji in Kuwait. Alpha Company commander Captain Michael Darst led tactical operations with the support of junior commissioned officers and senior enlisted noncommissioned officers in rapidly decimating Iraqi ground forces and forged a path to Kuwait City in the opening hours of Operation Desert Storm. Coming at the end of Darst's service, his enviable career in the Marine Corps ended as quickly as Operation Desert Storm.

Michael's great-grandfather, five generations earlier, was killed in the Alamo in 1836 at the ripe age of forty-three. Darst had privately believed himself to be a Texan first and CEO second. His family, after all, had sacrificed multiple generations of its best to the protection of Texas. The succeeding generation of the Alamo defenders had among it the son of Jeremy Darst, Matthew. Described by many as a calm yet violent fellow, Matthew spent a decade and a half with a Ranging Company, a precursor to the Texas Rangers. Two generations later, Collin Darst answered the call to join the Texas Rangers and was assigned to a company posted in Fredericksburg, where Comanches continually preyed upon the most remote German settlors, drawing Rangers out into disastrous ambushes. An ambush was, in fact, the cause of Collin's death which served only to feed Darst family traditions surrounding Texas and its unique development.

Michael and Sue met on a blind date during rush week at Texas Christian University and they dated throughout their college days. Sue painted, had an eye for colors and statements, and gave Michael three beautiful children—one older boy and two sisters. He signed a contract with the Marines and began the ten-week officer candidate school after his junior year at TCU. Darst found a home in the Corps, and he was promoted to captain just prior to the build up around Operation Desert Storm.

After Desert Storm, Michael returned home to Sue and their three young children and he entered the business world with a regional energy company in Lafayette, Louisiana as a mid-level manager.

As Darst predicted, Charlie drove up on Demitri Riojas nearly two miles west of Cuero on highway 72 just past the livestock auction. Demi's smile, albeit genuine, was reserved for his brothers, and his gentle nature was an alternate ego to the quiet but deadly warfighter who demonstrated unbridled ruthlessness to Taliban. He swung a large, overfilled duffle into the bed of the truck, hopped into the truck and said, "Afternoon, sir."

Charlie smiled and said, "Good afternoon. Thanks for playing along. If you'll be so kind as to hand me one of the burner phones, I need to text Mr. Darst about my dog." They exchanged smiles and Charlie began to feel that they would somehow get clear of all the mess.

Darst breathed a small sigh after receiving the text about Jolie, and he studied the Baker .625 caliber flintlock rifle hanging below the portrait of his beloved ancestor who gave the ultimate sacrifice at the Mission San Antonio de Bexar in 1836. The convergence of current events had not gone unnoticed. The COVID ruse, the border chaos, the perverse and total corruption of DC, all came together in perfect harmony. He looked down at the toes of his crocodile boots then stepped over to the bar and pulled the top from a single malt and poured a generous double. He sipped and contemplated, all the while realizing the consequences for what would take place next could never be undone.

"Sue, hi hon, it's me," Darst said over the phone. "Yes, I'm about to head home. I don't know what you have planned tonight for dinner, but let's go out for a burger. Some stuff for us to kick around, ok? Good, I'll see you in a bit. I love you, too, Sue." He gulped the last of his glass and made his way out of the NRG building saying goodnight to security as he did every night. She won't remember a word. Damn it.

Meanwhile, very little was exchanged between O'Neal and Riojas until they approached the hospital parking lot, when Charlie said, "Ok, could you please jump in the back seat and keep low?" He found a parking place and texted Sophia of his arrival as he walked into the ER.

He spied Sophia down the long hallway in conversation with one of the doctors, who was a little more animated than a friendly chat. O'Neal continued to walk toward her. She looked at Charlie, said a few words to the doctor, and turned to walk toward Charlie. As always, they tightly hugged, kissed, and grabbed each other's hand as they walked out. She wrenched his hand unwilling to let go. He'd never seen her scared like this. Just reaching the parking lot, Charlie pulled Sophia close and whispered, "Don't look at my truck, and don't be surprised by the guy hunkered down in the back seat. His name is Demi, he is with NRG in Cuero, and Mr. Darst wants him to cover us for a few days."

"That doc I was talking to, the surgeon? He knows. And he knows I know," she whispered, her voice shaking. WTH?

When they returned home, he walked the dog several times around the block. But, not before drawing Sophia a very warm bath with salt crystals, gardenia, her favorite, and gently placing her in it. He picked up her bits of clothing, lit two candles, blew her a silent kiss, and turned out the bathroom light. She needed a fetal moment in private.

Later that week, Sophia and Charlie drove a short way to meet Michael and Sue Darst at Brennan's Restaurant in Houston. Everyone blended smoothly, and the two wives got along like they were already friends catching up. Their general conversation dwelled mostly on the Centers for Disease Control, COVID-19, and Sophia's hospital.

Sophia lamented the heightened protocols, which prevented her senior parents from flying in for the holidays. "They haven't gotten sick yet. I say 'yet' because no one really knows what it is. And, miraculously the flu has completely gone away. I think there were two cases in the hospital last week. It's the respirators, stupid."

Charlie touched her hand, and their eyes met. He handed her a menu and whispered, "They have the grilled artichokes that you love."

Her suspicion of the rapidly developed vaccines and the reporting inconsistencies had soared, and the hospital staff displayed paranoid behavior when any resistance to instructions from on high and not executed without question became items on personnel performance records. Fear and anxiety were slowly but steadily rising throughout the ranks and Sophia's anger grew with it.

That night, when they walked into the restaurant, O'Neal firmly grabbed Sophia's arm, spun her toward him and he reached in for a kiss. Sophia looked up at Charlie with calm, reassuring eyes. "It's all good. We got it all."

"I am so proud of you, Charles O'Neal. Would you marry me?"

"I'll have to ask my wife," O'Neal responded, and they laughed as they walked into the dining room hand in hand.

Michael Darst rose as the O'Neals approached the table and Sue Darst then stood up, shook Sophia's hand, and hugged her saying, "Sophia, I'm so glad to finally meet you!" Her purposeful eye contact with Sophia left no question that it was heartfelt. Charlie rounded the table, extending his hand to Sue, and genuflected ever so slightly. On cue, the waiter reached the table as napkins reached their laps. A lengthy welcome and introduction was immediately followed by adult drink orders and a run-down of the special entrees. Michael reminded the party of Brennan's infamous turtle soup, and the two couples laughed.

"So," said Sue, "Michael tells me you work at one of my favorite places."

Sophia, looking confused said, "Well, I work at the Regional Hospital."

"I'm sure you're familiar with the recently expanded pediatric unit there, the Stork Unit?" asked Sue.

"Yes, well, of course." Sophia laughed. She sparkled that evening. Healthy, happy, what more could a man ask for?

"Well, the handsome man to my left was able to provide over four million dollars for that wing by arm-twisting some of his counterparts in the energy business."

Darst smiled and took Sue's hand that was casually on the table. He smiled at Sophia and said, "It needed some inspirational architecture, and it was worth every dime. Sue did it all."

"I had no idea," said Sophia. "I love that building and now it seems even more spectacular, knowing that y'all made it happen." Sue excused herself and walked to the other side of the restaurant.

Charlie brought the conversation back to the table asking Sophia if she had glanced at the wine list. "Not yet."

"Do you like wine?" Darst asked her.

Sophia replied with a smile, "I never tasted wine, but I love the thought of it."

When she said that, Darst smiled, looked at Charlie and smiled again. Charlie perceived the expression as a silent sign of approval. Sue returned to the table, pale and glassy-eyed. She had changed. Michael leaned into Sue to ask if she had considered her menu choices, and she pushed the menu away as if to say she was no longer interested in eating.

"For the first time in decades," stated Sue to Sophia, "I won't be chairing the Charity Ball this year. My husband doesn't think I'm fit to do it. Don't be too surprised if he calls you to plead with you to co-chair it. It's one of the many thankless things we do for the men we love."

Darst turned to Charlie saying, "I really wanted our girls to meet, and I hope you and Sophia will stay and enjoy a great meal on me. Anything you want. Ok? I need to get Sue home."

"Sophia, I'm so glad to finally meet you," he said, "and I hope the next time we get together you'll share some insider scoop on the hospital just for fun? Please consider the turtle soup," he added, winked, and she waved. O'Neal stood to shake hands with the couple, who left at once and were gone. Charlie and Sophia were left alone to fine dine and share notes.

"I didn't see that coming," Sophia offered first.

"What did we just see?" asked Charlie.

"We just saw a woman with a hankering for prescription drugs," said Sophia.

Charlie and Sophia's return trip home that night was mostly in silence, sans the road noise, the radio providing distraction, occasionally hearing the other singing parts of old songs, and totally rewriting the refrains they hadn't heard for twenty years. They laughed easily and shared dessert and a cold beer once in a while. Almost an hour passed when Sophia slowly looked at him causing him to take his eyes off the road. With the fecundity of wild deer this year, he had to remain vigilant. Sophia just blurted out, "I'm so sorry, I'm so sorry. Please forgive me, Charlie."

"It's ok, Sophia, do you want me to pull off the road? Here up the road. Hang on. We'll get through this."

He heard her say, "It's too late," as he parked the truck and looked at her.

"No." Sophia sat there, silent, head down, tears running down her face. "You don't understand."

"Sophia, what are you talking about? What don't I understand?" Charlie looked deeply into her eyes; her nose was running. "What is it, my darling?"

"They forced me to take it," she spoke.

"Who did? Take what?" Charlie was frozen, unable to breathe. His mind raced with fear then anger as he grabbed her arm. "What do you mean? That wasn't the plan, our plan. Oh no…" He hit the steering wheel pretty hard and looked into her eyes. "Tell me you quit."

"No, Charlie. You know I couldn't do that. I would never work again if I did that. My reputation, after all. There are consequences for rash behavior. Besides, I can't quit, I have a fellowship for eighteen more months. I've worked my whole life for this. I'd work seven days a week, if someone asked me to. We've received more new cases today than all last week. I'm needed more than ever. We've been told that all accumulated holidays and sick pay days have now been canceled until further notice."

Charlie recoiled. "You could have quit, taken leave. Something."

"They need me."

"They need you? They? Who's they? I need you, your husband, I need you alive."

"I've done a terrible thing. Please, please, forgive me."

O'Neal eased the truck back onto the highway and silence again claimed the truck's interior. They lay in bed that night, Charlie a bit rigid, numb, resisting revisiting dinner. He didn't feel anything. He tried but he might as well be dead. He closed his eyes and remembered falling from the sky. He jolted, he was disoriented, angry, crying.

Five weeks later, Sophia would be dead. And, yes, she was pregnant.

Chapter 3

Sophia often said, "You never see the bus that hits you. And, in her case, nothing could be truer. She and Charlie wrestled over the possible ill-effects the COVID vaccine could bring. Charlie raced home in the evenings, not to get away from work but to be with Sophia, who generally would have finished her duties at the hospital and arrived home well before Charlie. Daily, he studied her for any change she might exhibit, however slight.

The occasional lingering scent of "hummingbird food," as Charlie called it, permeated the air in the living room, and it made him smile to know that Sophia was in a creative way, probably painting her next piece. It would only be minutes later that he could reunite with her, the love of his life. Her hummingbird food, the cannabis flower, wasn't Charlie's cup of tea. But he loved their conversations that ranged from international politics to history to church doctrine. She was macro. Sophia often shared with him stories of such detail and content that he would be thinking in sheer wonder how she would bring it all together in a rational and cogent manner, to his delight. Charlie had seen so much chaos and death in the middle east that the times Sophia and he drifted off into long conversations proved to be anesthesia and he loved the journeys they experienced while never leaving the master en suite.

One evening after a romantic bath, Sophia turned to Charlie, complaining of extreme dizziness, which quickly led to nausea and vomiting. Wasting no time, Charlie dressed Sophia in tights and sweatshirt and rushed her to the emergency room. The doctors worked for hours to correct her dropping blood pressure and arrhythmia, or erratic pulse, to no avail.

Charlie waited for hours and when the doctor and lead nurse entered the waiting room, their expressions alone delivered the worst news of O'Neal's life. His miracle once-in-a-lifetime lover was gone. The explanations were vague and generalized, almost unbelievable. They were lying. She just crashed? The emotion was overwhelming and downright raw.

For the hospital staff, the lifeless body of Sophia was just another day at the salt mine, business as usual. Sophia O'Neal, RN had died; complications of COVID-19.

In many ways, Sophia was the last person to be considered vulnerable to such a sudden death. She was the healthy one, the picky eater, the one fixing others, not the one needing healing. But for Charlie, the hummingbird had died. He was numb. He knew it. O'Neal knew she had been left to die, possibly asphyxiated; he just didn't know how. And who. He knew why.

The news of Sophia's passing swept through the hospital so quickly that Charlie became overwhelmed with sympathizers from within the hospital and throughout the community. Dozens of staff, physicians and nurses quietly gathered outside the ER waiting room in the vast hallway connecting the emergency services to the main hospital. Sobs and murmurs filled the hall as they waited for a chance to offer O'Neal their condolences. The neighbors prepared food and support. He needed everyone to go away for forty-eight hours. Arrangements? Even her parents were not able to travel during the lockdown. Sophia's folks were crushed by the loss and Charlie could barely lift his head.

"I'm so sorry, Mr. O'Neal," said one woman. "I'm Carol Hennesey, a friend of Sophia's here at the hospital. Sir, she was adored by everyone and respected too. I know this is a bad time, but Sophia and I talked about some things I found in the necropsy of COVID patients. I would like to share with you what we discussed when it's a better time."

"Carol," Charlie replied, "thank you. Sophia mentioned that y'all had talked and honestly, she knew that things were happening that shouldn't be. I would really like to sit down with you soon to talk it over, ok? I know the vaccine probably killed Sophia." Charlie paused, composing himself.

"Indirectly," she whispered.

He slowly looked up at Carol and finished, "Can you tell me what I have to do to get an autopsy performed on Sophia?"

"The order usually comes from the Justice of the Peace Office," Carol replied.

"Thanks, Carol. That's what I needed to know. Can I get your telephone number to meet with you sooner than later?"

"Here's my card," Carol said. "Please call me. This is a huge cover-up, Mr. O'Neal. There are many scared and compromised people here."

O'Neal managed a small smile. Although the swarm of mourners around O'Neal thickened the hallway, O'Neal felt himself losing touch with his surroundings and a strange sense of isolation overtook him. He began to desperately need air, and he banged open a push bar door to the outside gulping frantically to breathe. Then without warning the tears came.

A silent and destructive compound had found its way into Sophia in the form of the widely accepted chemical additive graphene dioxide, a component of the COVID vaccine she had received.

The 248-page patent for the Moderna technology that was administered to people in the COVID shots was filed in 2020. The patent listed several embodiments, or variations, of this technology. And while it was not known who received an embodiment, it was known that several different batch numbers were deployed. And some were far more deadly than others. According to the Moderna patent, this technology contained self-assembled nanoparticles. And in certain variations these nanoparticles could be used for the controlled release of compounds once they were in the human body. These lipid nanoparticles were encapsulated in polymer hydrogel, a controlled release coating that includes poly-vinyls.

In 2013, Dr. Ido Bachelet said that these nano robots had already been successfully developed in Israel. And that they could be injected into the body with a basic syringe. He showed an image of what they looked like, and they appeared to be the same structures that the Fifth Column found in their research and claimed was powered by 5G, which was confirmed by Dr. Ido Bachelet.

Dr. Bachelet stated, "My team developed nano-robots that carry antenna. These antennae are made from metal nanoparticles. Now the antenna enables the nanobots to respond to externally applied electromagnetic fields."

So, these versions of nanobots can actually be activated with a press of a button on a joystick. "The nano-robot we designed and fabricated is a machine that can be programmed to autonomously recognize target cells and deliver payloads to those cells."

So, the basic idea is to make a cage or a basket that protects a fragile, or toxic, or precious payload, and only releases it when it's at the right moment. ~ George Church

The nano-robot that we designed actually looks like an open-ended barrel or a clam-shell in DNA double helixes. In the absence of a special key, which is a molecule or protein, the duplexes are strong and hold the entire structure together. But when the key is present, DNA recognizes that key, and the duplex zips open.

The work of Todd Callender's team at *vaxxchoice.com* concluded that these shots contain a variety of synthetic pathogens that can be released by a madman using external 5G frequencies. The Moderna patent describes these nanoparticle mimics, which mimic the delivery of a variety of pathogens and lists over a hundred of them within the patent. And according to the work at vaxxchoice, these synthetic pathogens each have an IP address, they are catalogued by the Department of Energy, and they use Caesium-137, which we have been contaminated with from the environment, as a building block for their construction within our bodies using external frequency. And, if that isn't enough, their research shows that the Microsoft patent filed in 2020, 060606 cryptocurrency system using body activity data, is now in effect and that this technology is turning the human body into an antenna, which can output energy. Humans are being turned into batteries to fuel the digital A.I. prison that is being built around us. And if you choose not to comply, the technology includes a kill switch.

On November 18, 2020, a well-known German chemist and one of the EU's top graphene experts, Dr. Andreas Noack, was arrested by an armed police unit in the middle of his YouTube livestream. On November 26th, 2021, just hours after publishing this latest video about graphene oxide and graphene hydroxide, he died suddenly. In a video, he revealed that Dr. Pablo Campra Madrid from the University of Almeria had recently done a Micro-Raman spectroscopy study of the vaccine and had discovered that the graphene detected in the vaxx was not graphene oxide (GO) but graphene hydroxide (GHO), which is an extremely stable molecule that is not biodegradable, so it basically stays in your system for the rest of your life. If you're lucky, it's a long time.

This is very bad news for vaccine recipients, because he describes graphene hydroxide molecules as "the sharpest imaginable objects because they are only one atom layer thick…a huge molecule which is extremely sharp."

In other words, the graphene hydroxide molecules in the vaxx behave like nano razors that cut the epithelial lining of recipients' veins, which he believes is the cause of blood clots and the sudden deaths observed in so many top athletes, lately. He believes it's a case of "Russian Roulette," where the syringe administering the intramuscular injection will inadvertently pierce a vein, allowing the GHO to enter the bloodstream, slicing up the epithelia in the blood vessels of hapless recipients.

He said here, "Do you hit the vein or not? Does it stay in the muscle? Then it is less toxic. But if you hit a vein and the batches contain different amounts of GHO, then you have to know you are cutting people up from the inside." Sadly, he said most doctors are not familiar with these new nano materials and they have no idea of the damage they are doing to the human body and graphene hydroxide does not show up in toxicology tests. *You have to look for it.*

The crushing loss from Sophia's death removed any remnant of gentleness and compassion in Charlie O'Neal. The coming days were a blur of sympathetic visitors to Charlie's house, now a seemingly big open void. He avoided the master bath entirely, choosing to shower in the smaller guest bath. The bathtub that twisted their souls together over the years would not be used for years by O'Neal. The wake at Sophia's funeral tested Charlie, and he succumbed to the Irish whiskey to numb his mind. While he watched the ice cube surrender to the amber glass, Carol approached and finally sat down next to Charlie.

"Hi, Mr. O'Neal," she said.

"Hi, Carol, you can call me Charlie. Thanks for being here. And thanks for the little tip on the autopsy. I hope you didn't mind a second pathologist being brought in to assist on Sophia's autopsy?"

"Of course not. It was good to work with Dr. Allen and it helped remove any question on the results," said Carol. "Besides, it was too emotional for me to do. It's going to take a while." Her eyes welled up.

"What about the clots, Carol? How can we tie it all back to the vaccine?" asked Charlie.

"I'm not sure. There will be a ton of scrutiny when this eventually comes to light," Carol answered. "There hasn't been much time for the officials involved to develop any response at all."

Charlie paused. "Thanks also for allowing me to take the video of the procedure from the gallery. You have my word that I will keep it under wraps for as long as I can. The specimen is safe. For your own safety, make sure you have a copy of all the files somewhere safe, away from the hospital, ok?" He dropped his head. "Seeing those nasty clots being taken from her was very hard to watch."

Carol smiled and rubbed Charlie on the arm. "I hope you're going to be ok."

"Eventually," O'Neal replied.

Predictably, O'Neal turned to his work to keep the pain of loss at bay. Mostly, Charlie found his situation tolerable and only on occasion would the Irish whiskey tap into his deep sorrow. In those times, he would be on the back porch in the growing darkness, sobbing and cursing. Sometimes the Irish filled the hole, sometimes not. He would always get up the next morning, get himself together, and work like it was his last day on earth.

Charlie occasionally invited Darst to join him in the boat to duck hunt, fish, or both. The two, along with Charlie's retriever Jolie, would find themselves huddled behind some freshly cut brush, sitting on folding stools, looking out over a few dozen softly bobbing decoys inviting a party for unsuspecting passersby from across the bay. Talk bounced from Texas politics to fish recipes, which would be quickly silenced when ducks feigned interest in the decoy spread. The many common interests of O'Neal and Darst naturally fueled a strong and determined friendship which would later translate into a life-saving bond for both.

In 2020, Amazon, CBRE, Tesla, HP, and Oracle moved to or expanded their operations in Texas. O'Neal had overtly built relationships at HP and had created a shadow team of multi-disciplined experts whose political convictions did not comport with the vast majority of HP employees on the sprawling Austin campus. In his official capacity, O'Neal was inserted into the most sensitive areas of Motorola, Oracle, Dell, and several other campuses in and around Austin. The knowledge Charlie O'Neal carried between his ears was highly sought after by executives and risk managers alike.

Walking the floors of several top-tier tech companies was somewhat interesting, and he chuckled to himself when he became aware of how transparent many technicians were regarding their classified assignments. He found that by appearing to show interest in a cable bundle or a control room he could, by listening, get a good understanding of some highly sensitive projects underway. The skill sets necessary to fill key leadership roles administering the state power grid, government IT systems, emergency services, transportation, and banking sat in cubicles sprinkled generously throughout. The big one, however, for Charlie, was the timed and complete takeover of the state IT architecture paired with a *temporary* impairment of all major cellular services. One without the other was only an inconvenience. The success of the instant momentum shift depended on statewide control of computer and telephone communication. The complexity nagged at Charlie, but these strolls through the bowels of the high-tech giants, all talent considered, gave him hope. Yet, only beautiful women made him sweat more.

His persistence eventually ruled, and as often happens with the most talented individuals in an organization, they are the first to go for the door when unpleasantries become increasingly unmanageable. Also true in this case, is the axiom that like minds think alike, and Janice Martin, a senior programmer, knew the analyst and the coding lead. Better yet, there was something the coding team lead was hiding and soon O'Neal learned from Janice that the coding lead, a brilliant fifty-year-old Stanford graduate named Ryan Becker, had accumulated a pile of shadowy debts from an online gambling spree gone horribly wrong.

A manageable balance of $55,000 became almost $400,000 in a matter of minutes and a couple of keystrokes. He was stunned that the knock on his apartment door came in only two days, but then

Becker stood toe to toe with a most serious and impatient front man for a Philippine media company who only cared about his employer's recompense. Gripped in fear, he called his close friend Janice in desperation for advice. This, of course, was the good news O'Neal needed to hear, and he quickly made the necessary arrangements for the Philippine company to quietly receive an acceptable but far lower settlement. Charlie called Janice and instructed her to, "Sit on this programmer, Becker, until I can get there." When O'Neal reached the apartment complex, he parked on the street opposing him and met Janice before they entered the apartment of the terrified programmer.

"Let's assume he's shaken up and he could try to defend himself, ok? So give him a jingle and tell him you have some good news but need to tell him in person," Charlie instructed Janice. "I'll be right behind you so just step aside and don't say a word."

As if rehearsed a dozen times, the pair approached the programmer's door and in an instant it was Charlie toe to toe with the shaken and scared IT genius from California. Charlie had never seen a grown man sob so pathetically and he bit his lip to hold back a tidal wave of anger that overcame him. He breathed, and in a manner of minutes the programmer knew that he owed his entire career and reputation to the man in his living room. A man who made his worst nightmare disappear.

Janice rose to leave at Charlie's signal-motion at the door, and Charlie, turning to the shaken fellow, held out a burner phone and said, "Ryan, take this phone. Don't use it or share it with anyone. That will definitely get you killed. You will hear from me, ok? Answer the phone once you see a ten-second call back. You get your schyte together for the next day or two, and do not speak to anyone but me, got it?" His nod of understanding spoke volumes. "Eat a couple of hard-boiled eggs today. That'll restart your brain. And take a shower. Any questions? No? Great."

Closing his car door, O'Neal took a deep breath, dropped his chin and offered thanks to God for a lynchpin in the process of turning the leviathan in his way. Lord, I would drop to my knees to thank you for guiding this hunt if they didn't hurt so bad.

"A wise General makes a point of foraging on the enemy. One cartload of the enemy's provisions is equal to twenty of one's own..." according to Sun Tzu

The Gulfstream made its graceful final turn windward toward the private airstrip in Kinney County, Texas. O'Neal always felt a rush inside when an aircraft began its final descent, with memories of operations in his past. Darst, his two crewmembers, Riojas, Becker, and O'Neal were met by U.S. Congressman John Milton who was perched in the driver seat of a Ford Excursion, and Texas Lieutenant Governor David West, who was leaning against the vehicle. As the jet began to shut down its engines, Milton approached, grinning and upon reaching Darst, the two bear-hugged and shook each other.

Darst said, "John, I want to introduce to you Charlie O'Neal."

"So, this is Charlie," Milton replied. "Heard a good bit about you, young man. John Milton, a pleasure to make your acquaintance," he said, reaching out to shake O'Neal's hand.

"Mr. Darst has told me quite a bit about you too, Congressman," O'Neal replied.

"Please," quipped Milton, "call me John. And thank you for your service. Please meet David West. David, this is Charlie O'Neal. I want to show y'all around some before it gets dark, and we have a lot to discuss over the next day or so. Hop in. Charlie, sit up front. And don't mind the trash on the floorboard. You can't trust a man with a clean truck, you know."

Milton's ranch was in Kinney County, whose southwest corner consisted of approximately twenty miles of the border with Mexico and sat just east of Del Rio. Illegal immigration had been the largest problem since 2010 for the county of just over 3000 citizens. A relatively poor county, the alien trafficking has long overwhelmed local law enforcement and Milton recounted many of the changes experienced on his ranch to his guests stemming from the immigration. The caliche roads twisted and rose to a large, gazebo-like structure, which overlooked the meandering creek far below. Looking east, the views stretched for several miles of mesquite and prickly pear. It was quite a spread, primitive elegance. Not a cloud in the sky. It was cornflower blue.

Milton's staff had prepared a beautiful spread of hor d'oeuvres and were busy managing the fire that soon would be searing thick ribeye steaks. Already at the gazebo were two men and two women, all selected by Darst, Milton, and West to serve as leaders of the future republic, all possessing the requisite skills and relationships to successfully develop departments of defense, state, justice, health, and technology. Here, in a remote section of a remote southwest Texas county, were assembled a tiny group of nicely turned-out people whose collective industry, military and legal expertise, and patriotism was unequaled. Darst and Milton looked at each other and they smiled, realizing months of their diligent work had borne impressive fruit.

Introductions were dispensed, and after Milton sensed everyone had relaxed, he motioned them to the overlook point where he began the first of several brief and intense sermonettes.

"I'm not exactly sure what Michael has already told you, but due to the critical nature of the situation, forgive me for any redundancy. As y'all know, things are coming to a head regarding the heightened friction between Texas and the feds. The U.S. is being conquered from within, just as our forefathers warned, and there are states other than Texas that are making the early rumblings of secession. The referendum to allow Texas citizens to vote the issue was squashed by our own Republican party, but several lawmakers in Austin, David among them, have signed a Texas first pledge and you can bet our folks are keeping them apprised of our efforts, and they are onboard, and I must add, *very* enthusiastically.

"It's important to remember that they are politicians, like the passionless robotic tools you use to trim a shrub or dig a hole. Sorry, David. Frankly, we are the leaders we've been waiting for, and Texas needs your help. Y'all are great patriots, and we certainly will understand if you must bow out of what's about to be the most important time of this state and surely our lives," Milton said, nodding around the room. "God willing," he whispered aloud even though he was assuring his own heart and mind that he was called. That saving the republic was under God's protection and direction.

Gently rolling a small rock under his boot, Milton studied his glass of wine and continued. "I think y'all know my stance on the treatment Texas has received from the federal government, and I know that you have already gotten an earful from Michael. Things are moving fast, both in terms of local activity and government restrictions. Our strong conviction is that ninety percent of the citizenry will gladly comply with whomever has the power, and we are also convinced that Texas can and will out-smart and out-maneuver those ass-clowns in DC, doing so in a swift and bloodless manner. Vote with your feet. Everybody in DC knows the Texas contingency looks out for Texas before the country, and except for a few liberals from Dallas and Houston, they are on board. We are assembling the nucleus of a group that will, in the coming months and with God's help, reassert Texas' status as an independent nation. Your skills, experience and connections would give our group tremendous leverage, and we want to discuss all this with you while you are here. It goes without saying that this is a close hold, understood?"

The group all nodded in agreement and O'Neal and Benavides stared at each other, nodded, knowing that they had a lot to talk about as soon as they could get away.

The congressman quipped, "Ok, enough of that. Raul, please lead us in the blessing?"

The evening was laughter-filled and became a massive star-lit display of heavenly bodies and constellations usually unseen beyond light pollution. Stories of past hunts were described with much enthusiasm, which would be followed by laughs and a drink, only to be followed by another storyteller, a few fish stories, more laughter and more drink. Only after hours had passed and the starry wheel in the sky had shifted did Milton officially call it a night and they returned to the main lodge.

Predictably, O'Neal and Benevides found each other just far enough away from the lodge an hour after everyone turned in for the night. Conceptually in agreement, they pointed a finger at each other in a demand to remind the finger pointer of an aspect worthy of dissection and deemed critical. Hours passed as they bounced back and forth key points to commit to memory and the huge importance of the events and how their lives would be forever altered.

Charlie, upon returning to his room, quickly showered and fell to his knees. So much to consider and so much at stake, he felt a rush of energy and overwhelming gratitude that God had placed him in this very spot at this time in history. And how he wished Sophia could be here. His brain occasionally allowed him to think he smelled her perfume, as if she was in the room, which we all know she was not. He prayed for strength and discernment.

O'Neal turned toward the knock on his door and saw Darst fill his doorway.

"Do you have a minute?" Darst asked.

"Of course," O'Neal replied. "Come on in."

Darst dropped down into the overstuffed club chair and put his feet up on the ottoman opposite the small table and began. "I wanted to take a minute with you to clarify some things that you may be wondering about. You know me as well as anyone, and it probably won't surprise you that I have no intention of becoming the president of this new republic. On the other hand, David West does, and while he's far from perfect, he's our guy and he's got a pile of chits to cash in with the governor. Besides, I can do a lot more from the outside.

"David and John are well aware of how important you are to me, and John's bluntly told me you have free rein to do what you feel is best for the protection of Texas. You will be tested, and probably chastised, but if you just do the right thing, I guarantee you history will look kindly on you. Beyond Riojas, I know you'll have to build the other relationships. Officially, your role will have unique power and will wrestle with external and internal protection, and I can't imagine doing this without you. Unofficially, you will also work with Riojas and his teams to weed out the inevitable dissenters, once they cross the line to violence. In the end, you will have sacrificed much if not all, but for now you need to build an air-tight team. Come to me when you need to, ok?"

"Yessir, will do," replied O'Neal.

"And there's one more thing, Charlie. It's about my wife. I'm sure you and Sophia could see that she's struggling, and to make a long story short, she's not receptive to getting help. I fear that she's headed toward her own demise. I've done all that I can. It's a bad situation that I'm trying to segregate from this effort, which is so much larger than any one person. I know you talk to the Divine, Charlie. I've heard you. Maybe you could keep her in your prayers."

"Of course," said Charlie.

"Ok, then," said Darst, "I'll let you get some rest. Good night."

Charlie was moved by Michael's words and, yes, he would include Sue, and ask for wisdom to execute His plan.

The following morning, the faint sound of Conjunto music could be heard from the lodge kitchen, where Raul and Milton were watching the chef bring together a breakfast befitting a five-star restaurant. Flaco Jimenez' accordion enveloped the kitchen and dining areas, and a massive dining table was set for the straggling guests. As the congressman walked from guest to guest, he struck up a conversation that made each feel as though he was a lifelong friend. The topic of secession was always front and center, and Milton artfully responded that all the questions would be discussed after breakfast. Darst and O'Neal grinned at each other at the sight of the freshly baked tortillas, chorizo, and eggs, and Rio Grande grapefruit placed between them.

Milton again summoned Raul to offer the breakfast blessing. Afterward, the mostly silent room, sans kitchen noises, broke into song, with talk of bobwhite quail and whitetail deer. There was cohesion in the group, fit, smart, patriotic. They laughed and told stories based in truth, exuded precision, and shared information and contacts readily. How did he get so damn lucky?

Seeing everyone pull away from their plate, Milton offered, "Please make yourself available here in a half hour. We'll have materials for you and please be absolutely sure your phones are off and secured in the faraday pouch. The first session will take at least three hours, maybe more."

The congressman, carrying multiple files and swigging the last of a coffee, found everyone in the lodge engaged in muffled, serious discussions simultaneously, which abruptly stopped as he joined them.

"Alright, ladies and gents, a few things to cover first regarding comms, and please remember, our goal is to lawfully and peacefully reassert Texas as a sovereign state, a constitutional republic. Historical truth has been expunged, sadly, and we have lost our character and our generational lore. We are Texas, damn it! So few understand that Texas was a damn sovereign country before it annexed the U.S. and became a state." He threw down his files and grabbed a chair. This guy was a rough rider… by blood.

"From now until then, you must presume that you are monitored in every sense. Cell phones, satellite imagery, drones, and even direct surveillance. Your personal devices are just that—*personal.* Continue to maintain your normal profiles and usage on your phones, your computers, etc. However, do not use these devices to communicate to anyone on this team for the purpose of our mission. You will be issued burner phones, faraday bags if you do not have one, and portable ham radios for our business only, and we'll get into that later. Also remember to use the faraday bags within one mile of this spot. We will soon provide instructions to manage connectivity between your personal devices and the outside world.

This protocol is absolute, understood?" Everyone knew and understood the serious nature.

"Regarding materials, there will be zero paper records held by anyone until further notice, understood?"

Milton then moved on to say, "David West, our lieutenant governor, and I, have spent countless hours in private conversation about some of the people and structures needed to be ready when this ship launches, and I'll let David fill you in. David, the floor is yours."

West offered a brief smile and walked to the front of the room. His hands behind his back, he faced the group and said, "You may or may not know this, but Governor Harper just successfully obtained a Statement of Mutual Cooperation with the U.K., Germany, and India over the last couple of days. The statements of mutual cooperation aren't a full trade deal because individual U.S. states do not have the power to sign those, but they do commit these countries and Texas to improve cooperation between businesses and tackle regulatory barriers to trade. Y'all do the math." Looks of astonishment filled the room. "You can see on the screen the proposed structure of the Republic of Texas, much of which is familiar, right?" West suggested, looking at the projected diagram on the wall.

"Co-equal branches, but with a very streamlined structure, by design," he continued. "Notice the limited Cabinet, not all the bullshit cabinets like education, housing and urban development, etc. Just the bare basics and nothing more. Believe me when I tell you, that we may need a wall around our entire perimeter to keep people out!" West exclaimed and everyone laughed. And then went silent.

"Y'all are here because you have an impeccable reputation and highly developed skill sets, you are highly respected in your field, and you also believe Texas should re-assert her sovereignty. Today, you will be able to get to know each other better and discuss at length any burning issues you have or foresee, with your peers. In a few minutes, in this meeting, you will be provided a chance to present your near-term strategies to begin the build-out of the department for which you are responsible. Once again, from memory, no notes or digital documents until the go-ahead has been given. And to answer a question you will be considering, yes, the original structures etched in parchment in Philadelphia are better than anything else conjured up by man subsequently. But the departments created were very different from today and I suggest you research this vigorously."

In the hours that followed, O'Neal, Becker, Garcia, Hemingway, and James introduced themselves, offered an impromptu curriculum vitae and in some cases even delivered a short synopsis of what their department might resemble. Congressman Milton subtly guided the group through several hours of vision casting, but was quick to interrupt a member when an overly ambitious strategy emerged that could eventually morph into a thief-dom.

Informal teaming developed among the cabinet members, notably occurring when feasible optimal solutions were delivered in a blended effort. Becker became quickly stretched as the realm of technology was immediately found critical to the needs of defense and justice.

Before lunch was served, Becker began to show signs of stress to O'Neal. The new demands suddenly dumped on him caused his throat to become completely blotched and he was sweating profusely and nervously chewing his bottom lip. O'Neal found an opportunity to pull him aside during a break to remind Becker that he wouldn't have to pull on the rope alone and to focus his energy on the personnel he would need to assemble in order to have the horsepower required. And to breathe.

Becker was an unimpressive fellow, over whose narrow shoulders was hung a somewhat wrinkled sports jacket and an old blue Brooks Brothers oxford button-down shirt. His six-foot frame resembled a clumsy shorebird, and the encouragement provided by O'Neal enabled Becker to regain his considerable functional ability. He strode briskly to the front of the room and instantly began reciting the specific technical framework of the existing State of Texas networks and those of the federal government, specifically the U.S. Department of Defense portal.

"Even the IRS, that is if anyone cared." Everyone laughed and embraced him.

Such was the technical depth and breadth of his rendition that Milton was prompted to stand up and state, "Very good, Mr. Becker. Clearly you have a strong grasp of the challenges we face, and we appreciate your enthusiasm," as he rolled his eyes with a grin. Becker smiled in relief and returned to his seat. This was the point when Becker launched, well, Becker. He went from hiding out from the mafia owing them a half million dollars, he can't remember why, to one of the inside guys of an entire country.

Milton then asked Elena Garcia to offer her comments to the group. She smiled and made her way to the front.

"Thanks, John," Garcia began. "It is a great privilege to be among you and to serve in this endeavor. While I do not know some of you very well, I look forward to working with you in sharing our vision with the Hispanics in our state and bringing them alongside. Also, our relationship with Mexico will be critical to facilitate a flourishing trade partner and improve the border situation."

Elena smiled again at Milton and returned to her seat.

O'Neal stood, gathered his thoughts, and strode to the lectern. His hands in his pockets, he cleared his throat and said, "I'm Charlie O'Neal from Edna, which is just outside of Victoria. I provide security to NRG and have experience from my service in the Army, specifically Rangers." Glancing at Darst, he said, "Mr. Darst has shown great leadership at NRG and has allowed me to grow professionally and expand spiritually. I won't get too personal here, but I lost my wife to an over-reaching bureaucracy that convinced her to get the COVID vax and it killed her." O'Neal took a breath and continued saying, "As a sovereign nation, we must first enforce complete border security and simultaneously deport every illegal we can get our hands on. If they came across the Rio Grande, they'll be dropped back on the other side with the protection of our special forces. We will root out all cartel factions within our boundary and hand them over to Ms. James and her group to prosecute. If the cartels want to push back, we will insert teams in their homes and kill them all where they sleep. We have the will, the technology, and the resources to fully accomplish this. Our plan includes the short-term leasing of the existing U.S. government compounds to gather illegals and ship them directly from there. Thanks."

Laci James, an Austin attorney, was well known and perhaps represented best the fledgling cabinet. A University of Texas Law School product, James successfully litigated many cases at both the Texas State and U.S. Supreme Courts. Her legal mind was regarded by the community as among the very best and she was a battle-proven attorney and mother of three. A no-nonsense and mature professional, James reminded one of a former high school gymnast, trim and athletic. She moved quickly and effortlessly, and her comments were directed at the recent abuse of lawfare in national politics and the broad-brush relaxation of sentencing in the court system. Her belief in stricter violent crimes sentencing and hard drug convictions caused Milton to loft a hearty "Amen." She stood quietly for several seconds. Then she said, "I solemnly swear that I will do all in my power to put this nasty abortion *business* to bed, pardon the pun, once and for all."

Every single person at that table, that morning, stood up and cheered, some with gratitude that a solution would finally even the word, no less the whole issue, find its proper, a less prominent and outrageously insulting to all women, private, place in our country's lexicon.

Things were beginning to gin when Hemingway stood and slowly walked to the front of the room, where she also paused for some time, gathering her thoughts. Time had not been kind to Hemingway, her once graceful form somewhat worn. She looked through the room and individually at every face, finally reaching Darst's, when she smiled. With everyone's complete attention, she began by saying, "It struck me moments ago, that it must have been really a life-altering experience for those good patriots in that hot meeting hall in Philadelphia all those many years ago. Do you wonder how many of those remarkable people had the realization that they were on the cusp of changing the world forever? Or were they too close to the predicament, too worried of impending loss, too weary and hot, to grasp the importance?" Hemingway paused, her bright blue eyes twinkled, and she slowly stepped to a window, obviously demonstrating her statesmanship in prose. "It also struck me that our Heavenly Father placed me in this room as he did the patriots/rebels in Philadelphia. I never could have dreamed that I would have the honor and opportunity to be a part of a group of this caliber in a noble effort such as this. The stripes on my back come from business deal negotiations with Arab camel traders, Chinese chemical giants, and Venezuelan despots. I know deep inside me that these hard, rough experiences honed me for this, and I couldn't be more grateful. I am all in and I thank you.

Milton winked at Darst who simply smiled and looked down

"A leader leads by example, not by force." – Sun Tzu

Chapter 4

"May I speak with Penny Townsend?" O'Neal asked.

"One minute and I'll connect you," the operator said.

A raspy voice message recorder responded, "Hi, you have reached the office of Penny Townsend. I am unable to take your call but please leave your name and number and I'll return your call. Thank you."

"Hi, Penny, it's Charlie O'Neal from a few nights ago. Look, I know you probably think I ducked out on you, but that's not what happened. I'd like to explain and hope you will give me a ring. The number is seven one three, two four eight, seven eight four two. Bye, Penny."

He took a deep breath and pocketed the phone as he headed down to the lobby. O'Neal was driven to a store to replace his badly worn outfit then to the airport. Upon returning to Houston and once in the car with Darst, O'Neal handed Darst the unused cash, and they immediately began dissecting the abduction. After much deliberation, they created a short list of possible adversaries who would benefit from the failure of their secession movement. O'Neal sensed a significant increase in Darst's intensity. Darst briefed O'Neal on the team's status and reminded O'Neal that his role needed to be focused on the security piece. Leadership had now been bolstered and a new level of acceptance was being observed by many Texas legislators, offering increased hope to Darst and the movement. The attempted abduction of O'Neal served as notice to the group that the forces needing to maintain the status quo could be expected to do whatever was necessary.

A few days passed before O'Neal had reached the conclusion that Penny wasn't going to call him back. A persistent O'Neal dialed up the foundation and once again Penny's voice message instructed O'Neal to leave his name and number.

"Hi, Penny, it's Charlie O'Neal... *again.* I really hope you'll give me the chance to get together with you so that I can *try* to explain a few things. Anyway, I guess if I don't hear from you after this message, I won't bother you again. Seven one three, two four eight, seven eight four two. Take good care, Penny."

Mere seconds passed when O'Neal's phone buzzed of an incoming call from the Texas Policy Foundation. Charlie smiled, took a deep breath, and said, "Hello?"

"Charlie? It's Penny."

"Hi, Penny," said Charlie. "I'm glad to hear your voice. Penny, look, I'd like to explain my disappearance from the restaurant, but I think it would be best if I could tell you in person. And it is complicated. If you can give me a few minutes, I promise I'll try to make sense of it for you. Just say when and I'll drive up to Austin. Maybe we could grab a bite somewhere? How's that sound?"

"Charlie," said Penny, "I'm kind of relieved to hear your voice too. I suppose next Friday evening would work. I'm always interested in a good story. How would Friday work for you?"

"That would be fine," Charlie said, the grin pouring through on the phone. "I should be able to be there by seven or so. Would you mind shooting your address over?"

"Of course not," said Penny. "I'll see you then. Bye, Charlie."

"Goodbye to you, Penny," O'Neal replied.

One of Charlie's least favorite responsibilities was to fill a seat at the many charity events sponsored by NRG. Darst made it clear to O'Neal that he expected Charlie to make most, if not all, of the high-profile parties for more than a couple of reasons. First, Darst always grew more comfortable and secure with O'Neal close at hand in a large room full of drink-guzzling socialites. Second, Darst privately wanted to help O'Neal find an acceptable prospect to replace Sophia. And then there was the conversation that Darst and O'Neal enjoyed, conversation that softened the pretense of a marriage with Sue, who had become increasingly difficult to manage in a public setting.

Two days after O'Neal reconnected with Penny, he was armed and present at one of those major fundraisers for a hospital system in Austin. As Charlie entered the hotel's lobby, he wondered how many other men would be attending a function such as this one without a date. The main hallway led to the ballroom, which was pulling in the finely dressed couples by the dozen. O'Neal spied an alternate, less obvious entry to the left, and he stepped through the push-bar door to a vast array of elaborately set and adorned tables. He skirted the edge of the ballroom, eventually locating Darst, who was visiting with a couple between tables. Tucked under his cummerbund, Charlie's nine mm pistol seemed to ride somewhat uncomfortably, causing him to occasionally fidget to bring it into a more comfortable place above his right hip. Waving Charlie over, Darst introduced O'Neal to the couple and in a few minutes Darst excused himself and Charlie and they walked to a spot where they could talk privately. Darst reminded O'Neal of the handful of contacts he was to strengthen during the evening, pointing them out by sighting the wife or date wearing something big in addition to their hair, and very flashy, with particular attention in the direction of Representative Anderson and his *entourage* table.

Charlie tended to mill close to Darst during the typical pre-event socializing. The amount of pure, unvarnished ass-kissing Darst received at these functions always amazed O'Neal. "Ad nauseum," Darst would mumble. "Your time will come.

"No, thank you." Charlie would laugh.

To locate the nearest bar, Charlie turned his attention, and his eyes locked onto a tall, auburn-haired woman sporting a navy cocktail dress with a low-cut back. *That* must be Penny…

O'Neal turned back to Darst, who subtly signaled Charlie to replace his drink, to which Charlie grinned and gave a thumbs up. Turning again to the bar, Charlie saw Penny looking directly at him and without moving gave him a wink. He chuckled and returned the gesture while approaching Penny at the end of the bar.

"Of all the gin joints in this town, you had to pick this one?" Penny said, swirling the straw in her drink.

"I should have known this would be a party you'd attend," said Charlie.

"A girl has to make a living, Charlie," Penny quipped. "And all the big fish will be in this tank tonight."

"Good evening, Miss Townsend," interrupted Darst from out of nowhere. "I see you've met my good friend here, Mr. O'Neal?"

"Oh, good evening, Mr. Darst," replied Penny. "Yes." She blushed. "Thank you for being here. Have you caught up with Representative Anderson? He was asking for you."

"It's early, Penny," said Darst. "And as you know, Anderson will be much more useful later tonight once he's gotten in his cup."

"Well," said Penny, "I see that I'm keeping you fellows from the bar, and I do need to get back to my table. I'm hosting the keynote speaker, and I shouldn't leave him unattended. Perhaps we can visit later?"

"Let's do that," said Charlie.

Darst caught O'Neal's elbow and leaned into O'Neal's ear to say, "How do you know her?"

"Met her on a plane just before the incident in DC, and we were having a nice dinner before those pricks grabbed me the other day," O'Neal replied. "She's a cool lady, what I know about her, respected in DC, and she's loaded with contacts."

"She may be cool, and she is indeed connected, but rest assured that not all of her connections are friends of ours, if you catch my drift."

"Roger that, sir," O'Neal responded. As Darst turned to the busy ballroom to resume socializing, Charlie also turned and reached inside his jacket for his phone to text Penny. *How about a drink after the event tonight?*

Let's do that, she replied in her text. *We can Uber over to the apartment. I'll find my way to your table later—Enjoy!*

When the evening had grown old, Charlie and Penny carefully eased to the lobby and requested the Uber, which showed up in seconds. Charlie was taken aback as he walked with Penny, her five-foot ten-inch frame propped even higher with heels. She suddenly seemed striking, and he reeled when he helped Penny into the Uber and her Cartier perfume reached his nostrils again.

Her apartment was uniquely Austin, all chic and ultra-modern, the security guard an embodiment of a pansexual. *Could be a guy, could be a girl*, he thought. It made O'Neal chuckle, and Penny cast a harsh glance at him for his inelegant reaction. Reaching her door, they quickly fell into the kind of dialogue that was prematurely severed the first evening in the restaurant.

O'Neal slowly pulled a corner of his bow tie and unbuttoned the top stud while he checked out the finer details of Penny's living room. Photos of Penny with several different people were scattered throughout, some vacation shots, some that were all business, seashells and assorted central American artifacts. One photo caught his eye, and he tried to study it but not let on that it interested him. Penny and Lieutenant Governor West. He reached for a nearby picture instead and asked, "Where was this taken?"

Studying the photo, Penny pointed at it and said, "Snake River. That's a good fish, isn't it?" She had returned from her bedroom in leggings and a sweater, and Charlie was encouraged.

"Definitely," replied Charlie. He continued his exploration and noted a framed, handwritten letter to Penny from a girl named Isabella. The letter was thanking Penny for her work at Our Lady of Perpetual Light, where Isabella had been placed after a harsh, illegal immigration from El Salvador.

O'Neal then cooly said, "Look, Penny, at the restaurant the other night, I did not leave you. I was taken."

Penny stared into Charlie's eyes with a total lack of emotion. "What do you mean, taken?" she asked.

"Just that," replied Charlie. "I don't know exactly who took me, but I have an idea. It would be best if you didn't know any more. It sounds crazy, I know, but I hope you will understand. And please believe me, I will gladly fill you in as soon as I can."

Looking down, Penny had a look of indifference, maybe disbelief. O'Neal recognized the look, and he added, "Penny." She looked up at Charlie, waiting for more.

"You'll see, Penny, I promise," said Charlie.

"We'll see, Charlie."

Penny returned from the kitchen with two coffees, and as she handed a cup to O'Neal, the front door was banged on loud enough to be heard in the next county. O'Neal reached for his pistol and whispered to Penny, "Are you expecting anyone?" But before she could answer he signaled her to be quiet and pointed to the hallway heading to the bedrooms.

They ducked into a closet and slid in behind a rack of hanging clothes. O'Neal slowly unholstered his pistol and checked to ensure a round was chambered. Penny stared with huge eyes, her mouth agape. Charlie shushed her and smiled at her. He was totally energized and began to rapidly consider their options if the door was breached. Penny was breathing very fast and shallow, and Charlie whispered in her ear, "Relax, we'll be fine."

For what seemed like an hour, they stood motionless in the dark, cramped closet. As Penny became hot from the conditions and the stress, her perfume grew stronger, and Charlie breathed it in. Finally, O'Neal turned to her and whispered, "Ok, let's step out carefully, you follow me." Without hesitation, Penny grabbed O'Neal's belt loop from behind and the pair softly passed the hallway where O'Neal paused to peak around the corner with his pistol at low ready. Finding the door secure, he re-holstered and signed to Penny again to remain quiet.

Inching to the door, O'Neal put his ear near the wall just outside the doorframe to listen. At least two men were conversing in Spanish and O'Neal grimaced, knowing his Spanish should be stronger. He heard they were going to wait downstairs in the lobby and call the boss. Their departing footsteps and the elevator chime told O'Neal that they would likely go down in the elevator, he hoped. O'Neal again motioned Penny back to the far end of the apartment.

"Penny," Charlie asked, "Tell me what you can about the stairwell and if there is a side door. Quickly!"

Penny fretfully clasped her hands together and said, "Well, there's a stairway on both ends of the floor, but the one near us goes outside to the pool area. The stairway on the other end has a door that opens to the street."

"Perfect," said O'Neal. "I'm taking you with me."

"You're damn right you are," Penny exclaimed in a whisper. "And who the hell are these guys?"

"Sorry that I brought this to your doorstep, Penny," O'Neal replied. "I promise I'll give you the details later."

I don't know about all of this," she said quaking.

"Hold on. We're going to get to the street, cross it, and get a car to take us out of here. Grab your phone, keys, and purse. We won't be back here soon."

After O'Neal peaked down the hallway in both directions, they raced to the far stairway and quietly opened and closed the door. O'Neal re-acquired a handle on his pistol as they made their way down to the exit. With caution, he led Penny out, across the street to the next block, under the streetlights to another building where he dialed an Uber. O'Neal checked his watch, and the couple tucked themselves in a shadowy corner outcropping to reduce their profile.

"Why does this have to happen to me?" Penny said to herself.

"It'll be fine, Penny," O'Neal promised.

Charlie dialed Demi's cell, and he told the whole story to Demi, who volunteered to drive to Charlie's house and check the property for any visitors. O'Neal was quite aware that this was one of Demi's favorite things to do, like some people anticipate a camping trip.

As they approached the parking garage to O'Neal's truck, he paused and turned to Penny to ask, "Are you ok?" She nodded and took a long, deep breath. "If it's clear, we'll get in my truck and…" O'Neal began.

"You drive a truck?" she asked.

"That's right, a truck," he said. "Anyway, if it's clear, we'll get in my *truck* and we'll get you to the house where I can keep an eye on you." He winked. It made Penny unsure.

The adrenaline surge following a high-intensity event tended to give him a cotton mouth, and always keeping a case of bottled water in his truck allowed him to drain a few before they even reached the city limits of Austin. For two hours, O'Neal carefully but vaguely recanted his experience from the back of the restaurant to his return to Houston. Hand-picking details, he stuck his wrist out to Penny for her to see the cuts and abrasions still glaring from the duct tape.

Charlie described the essence of a project Darst had dropped in his lap that involved very sensitive information regarding some very senior politicians. He steered clear of the topic of secession but explained that there existed a complicated relationship between Darst and Representative Milton. Penny was silent. Further, Charlie explained, the border crisis had fueled a labor-related issue at an NRG facility, and Darst found it necessary to get Charlie directly involved. He wasn't sure she bought it.

"Why can't you tell me the whole truth?" Penny asked. "I'm disappointed that you apparently don't find me trustworthy. You got me into this, and it seems to me that I should know why my apartment door was almost kicked in. That could get me evicted."

O'Neal carefully considered his next words. Words once uttered, they would forever change how Penny would view Charlie forever. And how could he know to trust her? At the DC hotel restaurant, her eyes sparkled, her witty comments impacted him, and he remembered how thoughts of her helped him remain collected and confident even when lying on the floor bound by duct tape.

"Pull over at the next store," said Penny. "I'll get a ride back to Austin."

Highway 71 heading east from Austin held only moderate traffic as Charlie and Penny made their way into Bastrop, and the lights of a convenience store came into view. Penny turned to Charlie and pointed at the store for him to pull in. The pickup eased into a parking space and Charlie breathed deeply.

As he put the truck into park, O'Neal began, "Penny, listen, the whole truth is that I am a small part of a team of Texans who are in the midst of a peaceful secession plan. We are all patriotic, well-meaning folks that have been called on to be a part of a once-in-a-lifetime opportunity to take back the sovereignty of Texas. We have had enough of the installed corrupt U.S. government running roughshod over us, and we are determined to legally take back the control. I have to trust that you will not go screaming to the press. You and I really don't know each other very well, but I can tell you are a very smart woman. It's not my nature to share too much personally, but I lost my wife a couple of years ago to the MRNA vaccine and I haven't even had a tiny amount of interest in any women—until now. And I really don't want to see you get hurt, so it is important that you let me take care of you, at least for a while, ok?"

Charlie intended to grab a coffee inside the store, and he motioned for Penny to come in with him. Penny sat motionless but stared at Charlie as he came around to open her door. He extended his hand for Penny's. Without losing eye contact, she took his hand and slid out of the passenger seat and the two stood face-to-face, her hand clenching his. Turning to the store, Charlie led her by hand to the coffee counter. Her grip tightened around Charlie's hand.

“Would you like anything?” Charlie asked.

“Thanks, I think I need a cup too,” she said as she reached for a cup to fill.

Charlie watched Penny fill the cup about two-thirds full and then grab a handful of creamers. *Just like Sophia,* Charlie thought. *How about that...*

Charlie opened the truck door for Penny, who wheeled around at the last minute and said, “How far is it to your house?”

“An hour or more,” replied O’Neal. “You are every bit of five foot ten, aren’t you?” he said as he stared into her bright blue eyes. “A long cool woman, eh?” Charlie said and smiled, then closed her door and walked around to the driver’s side door. *Damn.*

For the next hour, Penny relaxed somewhat and felt compelled to share with Charlie her own lengthy and difficult experiences with the governor.

“Charlie, since you haven’t mentioned the governor, please tell me that he isn’t involved with your group? He’s such a piece of shit,” Penny stated.

“You are right about him being a *shitbird,*” said Charlie. “He’s not part of the team, rest assured, but we need his resources and more than that, we need the power of his office. When this is all done, he’ll be invited to sit on the curb at Gitmo. Nobody wants to be associated with him. There’s a good rumor going around that he’s really gotten into buggering children now, especially little girls. We need to get some hard evidence of that, and I am saddled with that challenge."

"Maybe I can help. Are you familiar with Our Lady of Perpetual Light in Del Rio?" asked Penny.

"A little bit," offered Charlie, squelching a smile.

"I'm on their board," said Penny, "Along with some Laredo businessmen, a few church officials, a member of the governor's team, and Congresswoman Mays from Houston. It never made sense to me that the governor would take an interest in an NGO in Laredo. Why would he care? The only thing he seems to care about is seeing himself on TV. I recently found an irregularity in the financial statements, and I asked the congresswoman about it the other day in her office." Penny stopped; she fingered her hair away from her face. "She wouldn't talk about it and abruptly left the room. Her chief of staff, who I know from our days interning at *The Washington Post*, basically confirmed that there was two million dollars in un-documented revenue that somehow disappeared from the balance sheet. Although they certainly are taking many kids from the streets, the children are not accounted for any closer than their bank account. They have no idea where some of the children go from their campus in Laredo. The money, well that's one thing. But the children, that's so scary. It all stinks to high heavens."

"In your apartment," Charlie said, "I saw a picture of you and Lieutenant Gov. West. Tell me about him."

Penny's eyes brightened. "David West is a really good guy," she said. "He grew up and was educated on the east coast but has been in Houston for a long time. I think he was first a state rep, then senator. He was an early leader in the tea party, and his new wife just adores him. He's ambitious but pretty damn smart. And he hates Governor Harper."

"He sure might be the first president of the republic," O'Neal remarked. "That is until the first elections are held."

"Are you kidding me?" Penny asked. Her mind began to spin. There were many ways Penny knew to help the cause with West at the helm.

The two drove on in silence, into the darkness, steam lifting from the coffee and occasional sprinklings of rain welcoming them to the coastal bend. He reached over the console that separated them and found her hand already resting there, patiently waiting for the first time, the very moment, the spark, the trigger that sets it all in motion. Handholding has its own language, like grunting in the throes of lovemaking. She wanted to laugh out loud but bore down in the seat not to. "Charlie?" she broke that all up. "I couldn't help noticing that you must have hurt your leg somehow?"

"Yeah, it shows sometimes, I guess. When I'm tired, mostly. Or running hard on it. I was shot in Afghanistan." He stopped and took a swig of his bitter black coffee. "Only by the grace of God, I made it home, just hours before all *shite* broke loose. I was lucky to make it out," O'Neal answered. "More than you wanted to know?"

"Sorry to bring it up," Penny quietly said. She squeezed his hand.

"No worries," replied Charlie and he squeezed hers back.

As O'Neal and Penny Townsend approached Victoria, O'Neal reached for his phone and shot a quick text to Demi Riojas.

"In Victoria, sitrep?"

"Good to go," replied Demi.

"Good copy," responded Charlie, and he closed the flip phone and looked at Penny. "We are cleared for landing," smirked Charlie.

"What's a sitrep?"

"Oh, uh, militarese for situation report."

Penny laughed. Even she didn't know why.

The truck radio seemed to grasp the lightened mood inside the pickup, and classic rock and roll tunes serenaded Penny and Charlie into Jackson County. Always the sheepdog, Charlie had carefully observed the sporadic traffic for the last hour to ensure they weren't followed, and once convinced, he found himself in a pickup truck with a gorgeous, intelligent woman who showed a propensity for adventure. He silently offered thanks to God as the Rolling Stones blasted out "Gimme Shelter."

"No Beatles," he requested.

"What?" She damn near fell out of the truck, Charlie later good-naturedly recounted to Darst.

The farm-to-market road leading to Charlie's house was like many in the area, slightly elevated from the drainage ditches and bordered by McCartney rose, the invasive, thorny shrub all too familiar to the rural Texas coastal bend. Mostly impenetrable, McCartney rose provided practical privacy fencing for hundreds of miles of the region's farm roads and it now assured Charlie that nothing other than a feral hog would be capable of approaching the pickup.

Charlie's house appeared to be occupied, as the porch and living room lights were both on. O'Neal slowly drove the truck around to the side of the house, which prevented the truck from being seen from the road.

"I hope you aren't allergic to dogs," Charlie offered. Better late than very late.

"I love dogs," Penny softly replied. "They give the most honest love on the planet."

They stepped out of the truck and Demi appeared instantly from the darkness.

"Welcome home," said Demi.

"Thanks, Demi, thanks for helping. Any problems? Did you feed the dog? Anything out of sorts?"

"Nope, all good." He stood there for a moment looking at the woman he'd brought home. "Are you going to introduce me?" Demi asked, looking at Penny who was a good five inches taller than him.

"Sorry about that," Charlie said. "This is Penny Townsend. Penny, please meet Demi Riojas. Penny will be staying with us for a while."

"Nice to meet you, Demi," said Penny, who extended her hand to Demi.

"You too," replied Demi. "That house could use a woman's touch. The back door is unlocked."

"Why is this happening to me?" whispered Penny to herself, as she meticulously studied O'Neal ambling to the door, carrying with him an air of confidence and purpose. "I went to a dance and simply vaporized."

From nowhere, Jolie, Charlie's retriever, excitedly greeted Penny, her tail almost breaking in two. Penny reached down and gave the labrador a vigorous rubbing which instantly gained the dog's adoration.

"That's Jolie," remarked Charlie. "I'll show you around. Jolie, leave her alone."

Charlie held the door for Penny, who stepped into the house well aware that her story had just taken an enormous twist. She was stepping into the proverbial rabbit hole. There were antlers everywhere, stuffed and otherwise. Charlie was quick to let his hand slip around Penny's lower back, guiding her through the tiny farmhouse like it was a grand tour. He pointed out the bedroom she would camp out in, Charlie's, and he showed her where the fresh linens were tucked. He pulled a white terry robe from the closet and laid it across the bed, pulling the sale tags off.

"All I ask is that you let me, or Demi know if you need to venture outside," O'Neal said.

Penny nodded that she comprehended his request. She'd had body guards a few times in her life—to stave off kooks and lunatics. Not so much for her but for the company, her job included, she traveled with.

"There's cold bottled water in the fridge," he continued, "but our well water is really good here, so feel free to drink it. You should find everything you need in the bathroom. I also laid out some boxers and a T-shirt if you would like. We'll get you fixed up tomorrow, ok?"

"Well, it's goodnight, then," said Penny, and she stepped behind the bedroom door.

Demi and Charlie exchanged glances, Charlie shaking his head in regret. Demi pulled a beer from the refrigerator and Charlie grabbed a glass in one hand and the Irish whisky in the other. They collapsed into easy chairs and in silence recalled the day's events for several minutes before Charlie interrupted the silence by saying, "Demi, I can't thank you enough, brother."

"You're welcome, but you'd do it for me," Demi responded, shrugged, and air-toasted him, *Cheers!*

The two battle-tested men sat in silence again, as words weren't necessary for either to be comfortable. O'Neal would occasionally look at Demi, whose hands were clasped behind his head, his visible outer forearm boasting a nine-inch tattoo of the Virgin Mary. Hours passed as the two dozed in the easy chairs, Jolie at Charlie's feet, until the sun's light became too harsh to ignore.

When Penny exited the bedroom, she raised her nose to find the aroma of bacon frying had filled the house.

"Looks like someone got a good night's rest?" Charlie asked.

"I did, and I must say, that while I don't know what brand your bed is, I may have to buy one just like it," Penny remarked.

Chuckling, the woman and two men sat down to have coffee.

"I'm sorry to say, but Victoria is not Austin when it comes to women's clothes," said Charlie. "But if you will, just find all the things online that you need and share with Demi. He'll go to town and pick up everything. And Demi, please also get the stuff you need for a few days too, ok? And keep up your SA."

“Yep, will do,” said Demi.

O’Neal didn’t allow Penny to leave his sight for the next several hours. They talked about mundane matters for some time. She used to garden, and she missed it living in Austin in an apartment; he used to sky dive on the weekends, and he misses that, the freedom of gliding over, say, the desert, but being shot at too many times in the sky, put him off all of that. He doesn’t miss that. Soon enough the topic of government, politics, the media, black rock, and Hollywood all became fodder for hours of discussion that went into the night. That is where Sophia got off the bus and Penny got on it. She was not only physically beautiful, and emotionally stable, well-educated, well-read, well-traveled, and soft in a feminine way, but she was also looking at the world from a very similar lens. This was the partnership he always hoped to find, to know, trust, and rob banks with.

Charlie found Penny refreshing, and although she mostly spoke in a quiet, meted voice, she infrequently showed deep passion when children were discussed. Charlie guessed that Penny had been a presence on the basketball court at some point. A slip of the robe offered a peak at his boxers which looked great on her, he thought. Then it registered, it was a tattoo on her thigh—what was it?

O’Neal walked her out onto the back porch, and they sat on the lush patio couch facing the river.

"Would you like to take a short boat ride?" O'Neal asked. "I don't know if you've been in this area before, but it's beautiful out on the water, especially at dusk."

"Sure," Penny replied. "That sounds perfect. Do you think we could fish?

"I bet we can," Charlie reassured.

Charlie rummaged through his fishing gear, and once satisfied, returned inside to find Jolie and Penny in the house sitting on the floor in front of the couch, where Jolie was receiving a belly rub.

"Ok, you two," Charlie remarked, "let's hop in the boat."

At the modest boat dock was tied Charlie's boat, a typical center console, sixteen-foot bay boat. Jolie, well acquainted with the routine, needed no instructions as she jumped into the boat from the dock. Penny and Charlie laughed at Jolie's unsolicited action. Her tail wagged such that everyone knew she loved a boat ride.

The river soon gave way to the bay, which opened up before them as the small boat cut through the bay's light choppiness. Penny seemed to agree with the salty breeze. Her hair got all wild, and without make-up she looked fresh and untouched, an adolescent kissed by the sun. Charlie guided the boat to an underwater oyster reef known by the local fishermen to hold speckled trout and black drum. Charlie didn't outwardly show the pure pleasure he experienced when he was on the water. Inside, he was blissful.

As the small craft approached the hidden reef, the deceleration dropped the bow and following waves passed by the boat. Charlie killed the engine, walked to the bow and reached for the anchor, slowly dropping it to the floor of the bay some ten feet below. The peacefulness of the bay showed itself to Penny and Charlie in that moment, and they exchanged a long glance of shared understanding.

"How long were you married, Charlie?" Penny nonchalantly inquired.

"Over ten years," he answered. "Good years, really."

"Sorry that you lost her," Penny offered. "That was the stupidest thing I have ever said. You didn't *lose* her, like one would lose a penny."

Charlie smiled at Penny. "That's correct," was all he could think of saying.

"That's not exactly what I meant… Funny, I'm a little flustered."

"I'm a little giddy myself," he announced.

They both burst out laughing. They laughed for a long time. The clock was rolling back the years, and they were children again, out on the water, alone. Ok, alone with a dog.

They returned to the present and sat for a while, both considering the situation and how to move forward with what was shown. Charlie's thoughts were split among his safety concerns for Penny, his workload at NRG, and the need to get his group with Milton moving ahead. From Penny's perspective, life had suddenly become a dream, fully equipped with a life-size GI Joe doll. She wondered how many days she could evade her office without causing eyebrows to raise. She'd develop a plan, or so she thought.

Charlie offered Penny a rod and reel ready to test the presence of any hungry fish close to the boat. Penny looked over the reel, the lure at the end of the line, and without a word of instruction sent the bait twenty or more yards downwind.

"I will forgo the casting lesson," Charlie said with a smile.

The first dozen casts failed to produce any action, but soon Penny was successful in landing a nice black drum.

They celebrated Penny's effort and Charlie dropped the catch into the live water baitwell. His mind immediately began considering the pros and cons of the many ways to prepare drum, now that dinner was safely secured. Penny had already begun seeking her next victim. Charlie watched her and realized that the pleasantness of the moment was something he had not felt in years. The gentle waves slapped the starboard side, rocking the boat in an easy, loving manner. Jolie had gone to sleep much earlier, and Charlie was filled with renewed hope. The water always made him whole.

Penny and Charlie took one more fish from the bay, and he raised the anchor and restarted the motor to swing the boat back to the mouth of the river. Heading home, Charlie used much less speed, making the most of the ride back.

After the fish were cleaned, they returned inside, Charlie falling into an easy chair opposite the big screen on the wall. O'Neal grabbed the remote, and in an instant a cable news station brought the latest headlines. Several minutes passed with the less important nuggets of entertainment updates when the news cycle finally restarted.

The news of the sudden and mysterious death of Congresswoman Mays' chief of staff from Houston reached Penny in the bedroom and grabbed her by the throat. Amanda Johnson, a mother of four and former women's track phenom, had died from unknown causes. Penny rushed into the living room and froze, mouth agape, and began to cry and tremble in fear. Charlie, watching her, stood and grabbed her with both arms. Penny gasped for air and began to shake.

Charlie looked into her eyes. He knew the look of panic, of irrational and uncontrolled fear, of an ugly death, and Penny showed it all. In a flash, she became prey, and days would pass before Charlie fully understood that like following the death of Julius Caesar in Shakespeare's iconic passage, they would become the object of "The dogs of war."

Penny's visceral reaction to the news of Amanda's death lasted for what seemed like hours. Charlie learned of the deep connection between the two women, and that Ms. Townsend really knew a lot of very powerful people. And that she was a very important person in Texas; she just stayed out of the limelight, as much as possible, which gave her a large berth to navigate most effectively. He was not doing her any good service to get her embroiled in something that was hardly of her making and letting her get blown up because she was exposed unwittingly with a bunch of trouble-makers looking to steal back a nation from another nation with lots of explosives and shite. He felt a migraine coming on. He made a fresh pot of coffee, drank some, and brought a cup to Penny.

She was calm and composed, and happily received the coffee cup with both hands. "Mays did it. Or had it done." She got a strange look, stood and ran to the bathroom, where she threw up the coffee and took a shower.

Charlie knew she would rally, eventually. She had metal. The television blared in the background unnoticed as O'Neal dried her in new towels and held her in his arms, at times holding her entire being in his arms. He led her to the bed and gently kissed her face. Her eyes were swollen, and he gently lowered her to the pillow, like a hummingbird lights on a blossom. Their eyes were locked, and the outside world lifted and dissipated.

Chapter 5

Texas Governor Duane Harper, an autodidact politician, met the needs of both the Chamber of Commerce and the technology culture in Austin. A moderate Republican of the old school stripe, Harper found illegal immigration to be a tool with which he successfully courted both sides of the aisle in Austin and eventually, created a personal fortune. Though he vehemently denounced the horrors associated with illegal immigration publicly, he minimally resisted it from a practical perspective. Simply too much was gained by allowing business to maintain an effectively cheap labor pool, and the financial benefits eclipsed anything he could imagine.

Harper climbed the political ladder in Austin as many did, by ensuring his vast donor base of business owners benefitted from state policy that leaned gently their way. Policy that subtly took the form of deferred or reduced punitive action against violations relating to I-9 employees and counterfeit social security cards, or perhaps the convenient dismissal of worker compensation claims. Harper was *easy*, and he made sure his constituency knew it. The illegal immigrant business was booming, and he was in the catbird seat. The business of cargo logistics, as he would privately joke, was like picking money up off the ground.

Possessing an abnormally high level of paranoia, the governor built and maintained disciplined habits around his private, dark logistics enterprise, especially in communication methods. All his messaging would occur in a private retreat within the country club, all verbal in nature. Mexican cartel leadership of course also benefitted from his cautious practices, and they often expressed their gratitude with cash gifts that on their own made the governor's compensation look like spit money.

Laundering large currency amounts could prove a bit costly and time consuming, but Harper had anticipated the challenge and had acquired a modest vacation home in Panama several years prior to his election and very carefully took steps to avoid being lumped together with Yakuza crime bosses and kleptocrats in the aftermath of any Pandora Papers-type scandal. Physical transportation of U.S. currency was accomplished with little effort by palletizing and intermingling with office equipment shipments to Panama City. Only Governor Harper, his chief of staff, and his offshore banker had an inkling of Harper's vast cache.

The eldest son of a San Antonio banker, Duane Harper interned at his father's employer while in undergraduate studies. There he learned the methodology around money laundering, the characteristics that the bank looked for, and several case studies taught in anti-money laundering classes. It was also here that Harper began to see that banking was not his calling and law school seemed more attractive to him. The University of Texas law school accepted him and offered a serious scholarship, most certainly due to his father's long and deep banking relationship with the university and its chancellor. Postgraduate, he accepted a position with a preeminent litigation firm, and he wasted no time taking scalps—from the smallest contest to supporting senior partners on franchise case work.

The proverbial case of a lifetime showed itself to the Travis County district attorney's office when a major scandal broke involving a small-time CPA and his massage parlor chain client. During the discovery process, it became evident that the Catholic Diocese of Austin's Bishop had developed a sweet tooth for the Asian-American masseuse cadre. The rumors flooded the massage parlors and in fear, one of the masseuses trotted into the police precinct office and in an Academy Award-winning performance displayed multiple videos of His holiness playing the lead cowboy in rodeo-remakes, naked, wearing nothing but a pair of bloomers on his head. The district attorney, a home-grown Baptist, found warm comfort in the possibilities, and instantly assigned Harper to the case and redistributed his entire case load.

The virtually limitless budgetary powers of the DA's office and the Austin diocese produced a battle of titans, and the sensationalism brought to bear by the Austin American Statesman would have made Barnum and Bailey proud. It catapulted young Harper onto the cover of *Texas Monthly*. In less than a decade, Duane Harper rose from obscurity to solicitation by a trio of judges to succeed the retiring DA, of course involving an election whose outcome was predestined, given his commitment.

Although married, a disdain for women and alcohol made Harper a unique political force and allowed his focus to remain keen and temptations to a minimum. In a field of mediocre young Texan Republican politicians, the pathway to the governor's mansion was wide, straight, and unimpeded. The campaign donors, smelling an easy winner, lined up with sacks of money and Harper's future obligations mounted. Early in Harper's second term, at an annual council of governors, Harper received a last-minute invitation to meet with U.S. President Michael Robinson to discuss border issues. Harper, always looking for PR, excitedly but frantically gathered himself for the photo op two hours ahead. His abbreviated staff scurried about DC in search of the appropriate Texas bling and the preferred scotch of the white house occupant. On a personal level, Harper admired the charismatic style Robinson adeptly exploited to waltz into 1600 Pennsylvania, and although Harper sang the Republican song, he felt conservative policies to be almost entirely pious bullshit.

"Nice to finally meet you Governor," quipped the president shaking Harper's hand. "Can we get you something to drink? Maybe something to smoke?" Harper appeared a little stunned, that the president would be lighting up a bone in the oval office.

"Thank you, Mr. President, water would be great. I was thankful to receive your invitation to discuss the border."

"Have a seat." Robinson pointed to one of the classic upholstered chairs opposite the couch. A glass of water arrived on a tray with slices of various citrus, and the president nodded to the staffer saying, "Thanks and would you kindly turn on some jazz for us?" Within seconds, music filled the oval office, transforming it into a smoky downtown Memphis night club. The two politicos faced one another, Robinson toking and Harper struggling to calm his nerves. *How do they get the skunk stink out of this room?*

"Are you familiar with this technology?" asked Robinson while pointing to the ceiling. "It creates a secure environment, a low hanging cloud, for me to conduct completely secret conversations under. Nothing we say can be recorded. How about that? My chief of staff installed it one weekend. No one knows. So, now you have something on me. Anyway, it's regrettable that we haven't met prior to today," said the president. "But there's no time like the present," he bloviated. "And it's a perfect time for what *I* need now. It has been brought to my attention that you completely understand the dynamics around the border and know very well the players on both sides."

"I'm not sure about that," replied Harper. "It's somewhat complicated and does change quickly."

"You're being modest, and I hope you don't respond publicly in such a sheepish manner," interrupted Robinson. "From what I've been told, you are typically known to be statelier and more confident, am I right?"

The governor shrugged and admitted, "I suppose that's right."

"Well, there is much more for us to cover and unfortunately my schedule today doesn't allow me to push things back, so I'll get to it…suffice it to say I know all about your less public 'business' in Panama, and before you say anything, let me also say I couldn't care less about your personal ambitions. We all have them, so long as they don't interfere with mine. We also have requirements requiring a *properly managed* border, and it involves both public and private entities. That is what you can confidentially take away from our visit today. Let's get a couple of pics and trust me, you will hear from *us* soon."

The president and Governor Harper strolled out to the Rose Garden for the standard photo op conducted by the White House photographers. The White House Rose Garden borders the Oval Office and the West Wing of the White House in Washington, DC. The garden is approximately 125 feet long and sixty feet wide and is commonly used as a stage for receptions and media events due to its proximity to the White House.

It was established in 1913 by Ellen Louise Axson Wilson, wife of Woodrow Wilson. In 1935, President Franklin D. Roosevelt commissioned Frederick Law Olmsted Jr. to redesign the garden, and he installed cast iron furniture pieces. In 1961, during the John F. Kennedy administration, the garden was largely redesigned by Rachel Lambert Mellon concurrently with extensive repair work to the East Garden. Mellon created a space with a more defined central lawn, bordered by flower beds that were planted in a French formal garden style while largely using American botanical specimens. Individual plantings are changed frequently according to the wishes of the incumbent administration.

Harper was then escorted to his awaiting car and Robinson reentered the Oval Office. One of the unseen side doors immediately opened and Congresswoman Mays stepped into the office. "I heard everything," Mays exclaimed. "We can make him an asset." She then shifted and asked, "Mr. President, may I take a few minutes to discuss an ancillary matter, regarding one of the NGOs?"

"Of course," replied the president, who relit and was admiring the perfectly rolled joint in his right hand.

Congresswoman Mays nervously fanned the smoke away and leaned into the president and began, "The thing is, Mr. President, that there is a woman with the Texas Policy Foundation, Penny

Townsend, who has uncovered a major financial discrepancy at the Del Rio facility. She made a point to visit my office recently, where she asked me about it. Of course, I didn't get into it with her, but it may resurface, and I have a feeling that she could be a source of irritation to us."

"Tell me, Representative," responded Robinson, "how did she find this discrepancy, and what is her interest in the Del Rio facility?" His legs crossed, he very gently picked at a tiny piece of lint rising from his suit pants with his freshly manicured nails.

"Well," replied Mays, "she is on the board, and more importantly, she has personally become engaged in helping some of the girls find semi-permanent homes over the last few years. I suppose this is due to her soft heart or some other silliness."

Robinson contemplated his response, taking ample time to take a final draw on the cigarette. He rose from the couch and strolled to the Oval Office window where he crossed his arms.

"If this misstep on your part requires my attention, you should check yourself," the president stated, turning back to the congresswoman. "Make sure there are no other lurking issues, will you? I will make the necessary contact to adjust this woman's eagerness. What did you say her name was?"

"Penny Townsend," replied Mays.

"Alright, and, uh, what's your girl's name?" asked Robinson, as he scribbled on a note pad. "Please give me some good news and tell me the new deliveries have arrived below?"

"Yessir, the delivery is here," Mays responded. "Will you be ordering a pizza today, Mr. President?" Her question, of course, related to the selection from a never-ending flow of nameless, undocumented children peddled through DC for the pleasure of the elite and insane.

President Robinson would soon enlighten Governor Harper as to the broader enterprise. The safehouses, the lesser-known crossing points, the NGO-paid hotels were all tools to facilitate multiple revenue streams. Fentanyl and other drugs, of course, but the larger payoffs came from the safe transfer of humans in the form of terrorists and children. The poor asylum-seeker and hopeful migrant worker were of no consequence other than to provide a human river in which the more valuable human cargo drifted undetected into the U.S. The shadowy sponsors of terrorist and child trafficking were only too happy to pay everyone along the way and Robinson, with his hand out, was positioned to be handsomely paid and assured that the underground facilities would continue to be provided new, fresh sexual fodder for the hungry criminal elites on both sides of the aisle and both sides of the ocean.

An HHS whistleblower recently testified to Congress that "the U.S. government has become the middleman in a large-scale, multibillion-dollar, child-trafficking operation run by bad actors seeking to profit off the lives of children." Robinson was assuredly an active participant in the sick enterprise. His penchant for buggering young boys and his taste for cocaine and weed was known within wide DC circles. An eager and cooperative and dirty governor would make it all easier and would give Robinson an unsuspecting scapegoat if things quickly went south.

Robinson didn't feel the need to respond to Mays, and he simply walked her to the door, saying, "You should be more careful in the future, Representative Mays. This path is fraught with dangerous possibilities."

Later, after Governor Harper had left, or been dismissed, from the White House grounds, he was practically skipping. A few blocks away, Harper grabbed his staffer by the upper arm with a grip that left no mystery of its importance, and possibly a bruise or two.

"Marcos, get Jensen with the chamber on the phone, ok?

"Yessir, Governor," answered the baby-face staffer, who could pass for fifteen.

The genuine grins in the photos of both the president and governor, that popped into Texas newspapers the next day, were perhaps the first public glimpse into the real psyche of the up and coming "statesman," as well as the purported head of the entire mess. The snake from Austin had now found a way into a larger arena with much larger opportunities and scores more hapless victims.

Reliving the meeting in his head, Harper recalled, and grinned, at how he almost wet himself when the president asked him to *confidentially* help *him* with the imagery coming from the border, Texas being the largest border state, but in ways that surprised even him enough to almost gasp out loud.

Robinson was way more strategic than anyone would have ever thought. It would seem pedestrian that the president, of all people, would want a governor to produce some footage and messaging on keeping the southern border secure and how local sheriffs were successfully battling and arresting (albeit for five minutes) the drug cartels. But, to also want footage to encourage the Cartel community, however veiled, as a recruiting tool for cartels (and terrorists)—it was incredulous. Lawlessness didn't even begin to address it. He had no idea that Robinson would trust anyone, although the picture of his Panama warehouse was very nicely alluded to halfway into their brief conversation. Soft threat. Somewhat dampened by his past, Harper snatched up his ego, throwing caution and every ethical cell in his body and the tiny bit of everything else to the wind. Until he met up with someone wearing a badge, he was the law around there. Harper began working on the opportunity of a career.

All of the fifty Governors are involved with human trafficking—General Michael Flynn

The federal government pays the NGOs billions of taxpayer dollars through numerous federal departments—including Homeland Security, Health and Human Services, State, and Justice—for this migration weaponization used against America's interests. These NGOs and the Left hide behind faith-based organizations to keep their federal grants flowing and to distract from the horrific results in terms of human devastation, death, sex and human trafficking, forced child labor, national security and public safety threats, and more.

What started out decades ago as faith-based organizations supporting the State Department to resettle genuine refugees in the U.S. after a legitimate application process has evolved into mass illegal immigration and downstream activities, creating an immigration industrial complex worth billions of dollars. Worse, those same groups also advocate for more migration to the U.S. and against immigration enforcement. They claim they are merely helping vulnerable populations, but these NGOs clearly benefit financially from more immigration in this corrupt money-changing circle.

According to *Forbes*, Catholic Charities USA, the thirteenth-largest U.S. charity, last year received $1.4 billion of its total $4.6

billion in revenues from government support, compared with $1 billion in private donations and $2.2 billion in other income.

In 2021, the Lutheran Immigration and Refugee Service reported it received more than $93.1 million in U.S. government grants, and $23.2 million in church, foundation, corporate, and other contributions, making taxpayer-funded grants more than 80% of its total support. In fiscal year 2022, the DHS alone issued the Lutheran Immigration and Refugee Service a whopping $182.6 million in grants for unaccompanied alien children and refugee services.

Church World Service's, in 2022, received more than $20.5 million in the form of grant funds, and only $511,000 were from contributions. The New York City-based entity is a 501(c)(3) organization under the Internal Revenue Code, so it pays no federal income taxes, but it spent more than $3.7 million in advocacy and receives more than 40% of its assets from taxpayer-funded grants.

In 2021, HIAS (originally the Hebrew Immigrant Aid Society) reports it received more than $40.9 million in grants from the departments of Health and Human Services, State, and Homeland Security, compared with $46 million in contributions.

The U.S. Conference of Catholic Bishops' Migration and Refugee Services lists ten federal grants for migration and refugee services on its website, including eight from HHS (to provide services for newly arrived refugees; strengthen refugee marriage and families; unaccompanied alien children placement and reunification in the U.S.; a joint grant with Catholic Charities USA to provide training and assistance regarding human trafficking; a joint grant with the Lutheran group to address needs of refugee youth, children, and families, which was later supplemented to find homes for trafficked children; and another to provide services to adult trafficking victims); one State Department grant (resettlement services to newly arriving refugees); and one DHS grant (to process, receive, and place Cuban and Haitian parolees).

The southern border has become a conduit for homicidal cartels to illegally smuggle people from around the world by exploiting the loophole in our immigration law that allows minors and those who travel with minors to quickly enter the country. Some children are being "rented" by smugglers to help adult males easily cross the border and remain in the United States for years while they await their hearing. Children continue to be abandoned, abused, or face severe conditions once their purpose is served.

Migrant smuggling on the U.S. southern border has evolved over the past ten years from a scattered network of freelance "coyotes" into a multi-billion-dollar international business controlled by organized crime, including some of Mexico's most violent drug cartels. Title 42, the public health order introduced by the Trump administration at the beginning of the coronavirus pandemic, has authorized the immediate expulsion of those caught crossing the border illegally, allowing migrants to cross repeatedly in the hope of eventually succeeding. This has led to a substantial escalation in the number of migrant encounters on the border—1.7 million in fiscal 2021—and brisk business for smugglers. The coffers of churches, volunteers, social services and like agencies are swelling with donations making crime a very lucrative pastime, turning goodness and generosity into evil and theft, smuggling, kidnapping, assault, and death. How is this *help* helping??

In Uvalde, Texas, the small south Texas town that fell victim to the mass school shooting in May 2022, some school employees said they failed to take a lockdown *order* seriously during the shooting in May 2022 because so many previous lockdowns had been ordered when smugglers raced through the streets. The enterprises have teams specializing in logistics, transportation, surveillance, stash houses and accounting—all supporting an industry whose revenues have soared to an estimated $13 billion today from $500 million in 2018, according to Homeland Security Investigations.

Migrants are moved by plane, bus, and private vehicles. In some border regions, such as the Mexican state of Tamaulipas, smugglers affix color-coded bands to the wrists of migrants to designate that they belong to them and what services they are receiving. It is now impossible for an illegal immigrant to cross without paying a coyote connected to the Cartel del Noreste, a splinter of the Los Zetas syndicate. According to Craig Sawyer, a former Navy SEAL and founder of ***Veterans for Child Rescue***, the southwest border is "truly an invasion, but the humanitarian piece of it is just a smoke screen to keep you from looking behind the curtain to see what the cartels are doing, and what is this heinous and uncivil thing of child trafficking and sexual molestation?"

Sawyer said what's happening at the border is "being done on purpose," and masquerading the issue as a humanitarian crisis is a disservice to those trafficked and dying at the hands of the cartels through fentanyl overdoses and failed smuggling attempts.

The Robinson administration's open-border policies, operations, and use of NGOs clearly resulted in the mass trafficking of women and historic numbers of unaccompanied alien children. In its latest proposed asylum rule, "Circumvention of Lawful Pathways," it was noted that illegal aliens pay transnational criminal organizations "to coordinate and guide them along the final miles of their journey," adding: This cartel-controlled movement of people across the border is a billion-dollar criminal enterprise, in which the migrants pay thousands of dollars to be smuggled and the U.S. taxpayer pays billions of dollars to maintain.

In the words of a recently departed infamous State official, "The ignorant American people will pay for their own interment." (possibly paraphrased)

In the same breath, the administration described the role of NGOs "Both along the border and in the interior of the United States," as "Key partners, providing shelter and other key social services to migrants and facilitating the onward movement of those conditionally released from DHS custody." President Robinson, Representative Mays, and Governor Harper couldn't have agreed more.

The Heritage Foundation confirmed the onward movement of illegal aliens processed through southern border NGOs based on one month of phone-tracking data. In 2022, Heritage reported that approximately 30,000 aliens who traipsed through dozens of known NGOs, at or near the southern border, then traveled by bus, train or plane to every congressional district in at least the contiguous forty-eight states—including Martha's Vineyard. Many of those NGOs are from the same groups: for example, Catholic Charities, HIAS affiliate Jewish Family Services, and Lutheran Immigration and Refugee Service affiliate Refugee Services of Texas.

The notion that the humanitarian organizations have caused, to some extent, the increasing influx of migrants pouring in at the southern border has become a common narrative for years. The Heritage Foundation, for example, published a column in 2023 speculating that "it's not unreasonable to allege that the *administration* is paying NGOs to smuggle and traffic illegal aliens the final miles of their global trek." And in 2021, Todd Bensman of the Center for Immigration Policy offered similar ruminations in *The Federalist*. He wrote that "U.S. taxpayer's earned money is being [stolen and] spent in contravention of American immigration law and national interest in controlling the border against economic migration."

The U.S. government *does* financially support humanitarian outreach to migrants and asylum seekers, both on the U.S.-Mexico border and throughout Latin America. Actually, the world.

Under the direction of Texas Department of Human Services, cartels promise to get caught once in a while, a fake-random drug bust at the governor's behest. A small price to pay for carte blanche to corridors trafficking fentanyl, terrorists, human slaves, and indentured servants across the southern border and into the unforgiving Texas desert.

Governor Harper successfully promoted his pro-Texas policies of border enforcement and energy de-regulation, in theory and PSAs, but in the safe shadows he *bowed* to the left-leaning lunatic fringe segment of his most generous supporters, and under pressure, demanding a path to citizenship for whomever. The influx of immigrants, and the diverse, narcissistic, ignorant bullies who signed his paycheck at the Chamber of Commerce, the governor just wanted to hit pay dirt and leave town with a heavy suitcase. Ride off into the sunset. Like that.

Like many successful Austin Anglo businessmen, the governor often worshipped at the Berry Canyon Country Club, and it was there that employees and caddies served the wealthy and influential of Austin. Harper had well-placed contacts at Berry Canyon, and it required little effort to discreetly send or receive critical communications relating to the cartel. Two young Hispanic employees of the club were also on Harper's private payroll. Diverting Texas Department of Public Safety (DPS) Officers, through DPS leadership was simple and effective, requiring only twenty-four-hour notice for all non-emergency matters. If the governor needed to hear from his associates in Mexico on shorter notice, he would receive a confirmation of a lunch, dinner or tee time from the club.

Simultaneously, in Mexico, attacks and ambushes by gangs in Las Choapas, Agua Dulce, and Minatitlán were conducted with impunity, and information points to actual *cells* of assassins deployed by a GMO commanded by Nemesio Oseguera, El Mencho, who were reinforced by others from Orizaba and Nanchital. Pretty nasty stuff.

"The involvement of various law enforcement officers involved in criminal acts in Tamaulipas indicated that there has always been a certain type of protection for organized crime," stated a professor interviewed at George Mason University.

According to the Morena government in Tamaulipas, the CDN was soon likely to seek negotiations and protection agreements. Piedras Negras witnessed a useless *government special operation* that some said was all just for show, while others considered it a noteworthy effort. The events in question took place three years ago, and not many of the people interviewed had faith in the investigation's credibility. With just a few exceptions, the predominant opinion on the matter was one of disgust.

Critics of the special operation did, however, notice the advanced-looking GPS equipment that was in use, as well as the presence of a mobile lab to process information in real-time. While the marines seized the towns, and the army had all the exits, the federal and state police searched for functionaries and ex-functionaries, in order to take their statements. One of the spots that the sub-prosecutor inspected in Piedras Negras was the prison that is known across Mexico thanks to an incident in 2012 when 129 inmates escaped. According to witnesses, there were several Zeta "kitchens" inside this jail.

Some officials have speculated that the use of the "kitchen" extermination method has increased steadily since 2010, when seventy-two migrants, mostly Central and South Americans, were found shot to death and abandoned in a shed in San Fernando, Tamaulipas. The remains of dozens of others were discovered while excavating other secret burial sites. The San Fernando massacre put this region under international scrutiny and criminal organizations began increasing their use of diesel-filled drums to leave less evidence of killings and avoid any resulting scandals. Some would say there are 50,000 official deaths, but the facts would show that we are actually talking about, easily, a quarter of a million murders.

These massacres have not appeared in the news, but this is not because local journalists are ignoring the issue, according to an anonymous local. They had an idea of what was going on, but initiating an investigation—or worse, releasing the information — would have involved going into exile or certain death.

Zeta associates picked up dozens of people, all locally familiar, and took them to the ranches outside of the town. They also took night watchmen, cooks, maids, and chicken-coop caretakers—all of whom worked for the local families. The ranches, according to the sub-prosecutor's official investigation, were turned into an extermination camp, used by the Zetas to kill all the people they had captured by depositing their bodies in drums of diesel and incinerating them.

Anyone who shared any of these last names was in danger. Even the local public prosecutor, Blanca Garza, who bears no relation to the Garza Gaytán family, was forced to flee for a time. Some of the Garza Gaytán and Villanueva family members managed to escape and currently live in the U.S. Found were piles of empty five-gallon diesel containers and dozens of tires, which were used to facilitate combustion. These are the materials that are typically used by criminals to vanish their victims. One cartel soldier said, "It takes about half an hour to vanish someone, completely… They keep adding diesel until the flames have devoured you. When you see the fire start to die out, you just throw in another jug of fuel and off you go."

One cartel member, speaking anonymously, was quoted as saying, "The first time I was involved in this, I went a month without eating chicken or meat, because it smells exactly the same as when you walk past a restaurant or a place selling fried chicken. I realized that your average human smells exactly like roast chicken."

"The United States shall guarantee to every State in this Union a Republican Form of Government and shall protect each of them against Invasion; and on Application of the Legislature, or of the Executive (when the Legislature cannot be convened) against domestic Violence."

-- CONSTITUTION OF THE UNITED STATES ARTICLE 4, SECTION 4

Chapter 6

Charlie carefully studied Penny for any restless or awake activity, and seeing none, except her beautiful lady parts rising and falling with each easy breath, and wanting to stay fixed and just watch her, he stealthily slipped off the side of the bed to the floor, picking up his phone, confident that a day's worth of clean clothes sat behind the passenger seat of the truck. His shoes were by the front door. Shaved, showered, loved, he was taking on the day with a lot of might and a lot of gusto. "And just like Casper, the friendly ghost, *poof* and I'm gone," he told Penny when she inquired if there was anything out there about him that she needed to know. He glanced back at her and caught the silent twinkle of moonlit eyes, fixed.

She was awake, motionless, watching him, barely visible under the bamboo sheet, frozen, except for her eyelids. Charlie leaned in and slowly lifted the sheet to kiss her, and he saw a stunning tattoo of a single lily in bloom on her hip, with vine tentacles. It looked like it had just been plucked… His mouth was dry, and his heart was pumping away. He surrendered to what? Something. This feeling was different. Sometimes his eyes got all blurred and twitched, sort of.

"Be safe," she barely whispered.

"Shhh, sleep." O'Neal carefully slipped from the room, running his fingers through his hair like a fork, and flipped open his phone. He dialed Demi and routed around for a better description than "Dead Sexy." He spoke in a confidential whisper, "Hey, Demi, good morning. how's the shopping going?"

"Good-good, almost done," Demi answered. "Does she need girl stuff? What perfume does she like?"

"Never mind the girl stuff." O'Neil laughed.

"Are you ok?" Demi asked. "Are you sick? You got a funny voice."

"No, no." He cleared his voice. "I'm OK. Everything is fine." He laughed. "I have some personal stuff I have to get done today. Penny is going to sleep in. Just so you know where we are and what we're doing. I'll let you know if something changes."

"I'll do that." He laughed. "Text me when I should come back," said Demi.

"Ok, wait. What's a nice description. Dead Sexy but with some class?" Charlie could hear Demi smiling. He dropped his head.

"Freakin Gorgeous. Try dat." Demi dropped the phone laughing out loud.

O'Neal turned to watch the bedroom door as he dialed Michael Darst. "Michael? Hey, good morning. I was followed last night in Austin to Penny Townsend's apartment by at least two Latinos, likely a cartel. They tried kicking the door in but gave up and we were able to slip out and get back to my house with Demi's help to clear the area."

"Whoa, slow down. Any chance they were just following *her*?" Darst asked.

"I doubt it, I heard them reporting to someone over the phone that *thems* is lost," O'Neal explained.

"Ok, what's your situation now?" Darst inquired.

"Well, there's more," O'Neal continued. "Did you see that Representative Mays' chief of staff died mysteriously, of *unknown causes*, yesterday? She and Penny interned together at the *Washington Post*, of all places, eons ago. Well, she leaked some damning evidence to an unknown party and blew the whistle on Mays and her slightly illicit operation last week. She shared some intel with Penny, information that we don't have our hands on just yet."

"No, I did not know this. *What the hell*?" replied Darst. "Are you absolutely sure it doesn't involve Miss Townsend?"

A long silence followed. Darst scribbled some notes, and he finally said, "Charlie, you and I both know there are no coincidences. They are playing a zero-sum game, pure and simple. And they are using real bullets. See what you can find out. Miss Townsend is pretty forthcoming by reputation. She gets on with the folks. She could prove critical in helping us burn some of these criminal interlopers. Break a couple of fingers. Work fast, Charlie, we have a huge job looming in front of us. I know you probably want to grab a little downtime, you earned it, but thousands of people are depending on us to complete this mission. By the way, Penny sent me an email yesterday. If we campaign hard to get the referendum on the ballot, she wants to write for the cause. Slogans and press releases. That sort of stuff. That's good. You get her secured by someone else at some distance, and you get back here by tomorrow morning, good?"

"Understood," O'Neal responded.

"Be safe, Charlie."

Standing in front of a bookshelf teeming with books of every sort and mementos from around the world, Charlie folded his arms and considered the possible scenarios. Penny had to be relocated, secreted to somewhere close enough for a rescue but far enough away to lose the scent. His eyes stuck on an old family photo, taken when Charlie was in grade school. His sister Dana. Two hours away, always ready to defend Charlie. He flipped his phone open and dialed Dana.

"Dana, how's everything?" Charlie asked.

"Hi, Charlie. Good morning. What's up? Have you seen the news?" Dana responded. "Everything ok? Do you have a new phone number? I didn't recognize the number."

"Whoa! Too many questions. One at a time. Ready?"

"Very funny. Seriously."

"Things are ok, and yes, it's a new phone," Charlie replied. "I do need your help, though. It's about the Amanda Johnson thing. No, I do not know who did it, but a lovely woman named Penny Townsend needs a place to stay for a couple of days, maybe up to a few weeks, and I was wondering if you would mind letting her stay with you and Chuck?"

"Whatever you need," Dana replied.

"I need you and Chuck to know there is the possibility of danger. You'll love her," Charlie remarked.

"OMG, what's going on?" Dana asked. "And what's wrong with your voice?"

"I'll fill you in when we get there. Can we head your way?" asked Charlie.

"Sure," said Dana. "Of course. Coffee or tea?"

"Both, I think. She takes coffee with cream just like Sophia did."

"Drive safely. We look forward to seeing you both."

"Thanks, Dana. And tell Chuck I got a nice single malt from a friend for my birthday. I'll bring it."

"Yippee."

As O'Neal entered the bedroom, he found the bed made and the bathroom door closed. Returning to the kitchen, he poured Jolie's dinner and instructed her, "You get to come with us, duck dog." Jolie's ears dropped slightly, her eyes blinking her acknowledgment.

Penny appeared, donning her leggings, one of Charlie's work shirts and a cap proudly promoting a local concrete plant.

"How do you feel?" asked Charlie.

"What planet are we on?" Penny squinted her eyes at him. Then pulled down her Tiffany sunglasses.

A small smile crossed O'Neal's mouth. "Look, Penny, we've got to get you out of here before the 'unknowns' pick up your scent, and it won't be long; they'll come here sniffing around. Trust me, ma'am. There sure ain't another filly around these parts that looks like you. My sister in Houston has agreed to keep you warm, fed, and housed for a few days. Ya think y'all can handle that for a few?"

"Oh, no," Penny began.

"Oh, yes," he came back fast. "No discussion. We are leaving in fifteen minutes. You won't be looking over your shoulder there and you can go shopping. Just a few days. This phone has my number in it, and we'll not only stay in touch, but I'll come see you soon. I promise. But we need to leave, now."

"Are you sure?" Penny asked, tears forming.

Charlie shook his head to tell her that it had to be this way. He walked toward Penny, reached around her waist, and brought her close. Their embrace was long and tight.

O'Neal went through the house to check for anything she may have left behind. He grabbed a backpack from the closet and stuffed it with a Faraday bag, bottled water, a pocketknife, a flashlight, and some duct tape. He took her phone, zipped it in the side pocket of the backpack, and looked at Penny. Ready. Charlie texted Demi and Darst with a vague description of his intentions and they both responded with a "thumbs up" emoji. Jolie was loaded into the back seat, and they made their way to the highway.

The drive on State Highway 59 was completely second nature to O'Neal, having made the trip dozens of times on business. The sun began to set, and the local insects slammed into the windshield with increased frequency.

"Penny, I need your cell phone," commanded O'Neal, who stuck the phone in the enclosed Faraday bag. You can't turn this on, ok? I need to take it with me to Austin, but I'll get it back to you right away." He smiled. "Can you tell me what caused Amanda Johnson to suddenly die? Was she ill?" O'Neal asked.

Penny sighed deeply and replied, "I guess that Mays caught wind of her invitation to talk to Congress. She probably asked for immunity and Secret Service detail. She's had enough, that's all she said to me. She had gotcha evidence. And, she admitted to me that two million dollars had evaporated from the bank account of Our Lady of Perpetual Light. The non-profit in Del Rio is an organization that I support and fundraise tirelessly for scholarships throughout thc district."

"What do you mean you don't know where it went?" Charlie squinted his eyes at her. "Who else knows about this?" he asked.

"My boss knows. The thief knows. And you," said Penny.

"I need to make some calls," said O'Neal. "You can listen in if you care to, but you may be asked later to forget everything you heard." He shrugged and smiled.

Penny picked up the backpack and jammed it into a wedge between the seat and the truck door to create a makeshift pillow. Without a word, she nestled her head into the backpack and quickly fell asleep.

"Manny, it's Charlie. Hey, can you please give me a quick update on the status of the legislators on the list for Lieutenant Governor West?"

Manny Elizondo was on the list, a tenured Austin lobbyist, whose reputation was that of tenacity and a good understanding of where many *bones were buried* in and around the state capitol, and in and under several and various embassies throughout DC, Delaware, and Maryland. Lobbying is a major enterprise in Austin. Over $667 million was spent by lobbyist clients to influence lawmakers during the 2020 election cycle. Just imagine what the numbers are today, with the vast majority of that spending occurring while the Texas legislature was convened in 2019. *Yet only two percent of all those expenditures have a legislator's name attached to them.*

In the entire two-year cycle, only $12,944,291 ever made its way onto a detailed report filed with the Texas Ethics Commission. The lax requirements present plenty of loopholes for lobbyists to wine and dine lawmakers lavishly while remaining under the indictable limit. For example, a lobbyist could pick up the tab on $530 worth of drinks for four key legislators and never have to report who was there, why, or that the meeting even occurred. That's how a mere two percent of the money in lobbying ended up being associated with specific members of the Texas legislature. A donor who wants to contribute $100 to a legislator may not do so until thirty days after the session ends in late May. This is designed to prevent donors and PACs from currying favor with legislators while they are casting votes.

Lobbyists, however, may continue making expenditures of any amount to influence legislators during this time. The whole purpose of lobbyists is to represent another person or entity and to get paid to influence legislation. Influence is bribery. Or, used to be.

Lt. Governor West, Michael Darst, and Laci James knew the talents of Elizondo and knew of his dispassion for the U.S. government. Manny's family originated in the area around Mexico City, and his grandfather came to Texas in the 1920s to pick citrus in the Rio Grande Valley. Mr. Elizondo completed the immigration process to gain his citizenship. The Elizondo family had lost one of their men in World War II and one in Vietnam. The same government that freely served up their men to die in a far-off country was assisting millions of illegal immigrants to flow into Texas and steal jobs from the Elizondo family and neighbors.

"Hey, Mr. Charlie, how's it goin'?" replied Manny. "I had a long conversation just the other day with the Rep from Temple, the witch. Well, believe it or not, she is leaning our way, and I'll get her there, I think. Martin, in Tyler, maybe a lost cause, but I think we will have a new friend in Lufkin. The two from Bastrop and Bryan are solidly with us. Mark, the rep from Junction, is also in. Lubbock, Amarillo, and Wichita Falls are in process. Two mainstream Democrats in the Rio Grande valley are in play. I might be forgetting someone, I don't know. Is that what you're looking for?"

"Thanks, Manny. That is exactly what I needed to hear. If I can help with Amarillo, let me know. Laci can probably help with the rep from Temple. If memory serves, she knows her from school. There are some things I bet Lieutenant Governor West can do to help with the rep from Tyler, and I will follow up on that. Thanks for the update." O'Neal ended the call and dialed Darst.

"Michael, it's Charlie again, I just found out from Penny that two million dollars was missing from the Catholic NGO Penny worked with in Del Rio. Mays is on that board, Michael."

"We need to verify everything, Charlie," said Darst.

"That shouldn't be a problem if we can manage to keep Penny safe," O'Neal replied.

"Make sure of that, then," said Darst. "Let me know what you need. This is a huge break for us."

Almost halfway to Houston lies the small town of Hungerford, whose existence is owed to the railroad (tracks)introduced in the late 1800s. Café del Rey was locally recognized as the only restaurant in town that served real, homemade tortillas, and O'Neal was a big fan of Café del Rey.

As the pickup approached the town, Charlie asked "Are you hungry?" squeezing Penny's hand.

Penny turned to Charlie, pursed her lips, and replied, "Starving." And she squeezed his hand back.

O'Neal knew that he could easily pass for a local, probably not garnering a close look from anyone. But there happened to be a five-foot-ten-inch woman of striking beauty holding his hand. Anybody that cast more than a glance at Penny would remember her to the last detail. He sighed, caught her fragrance, and they walked into Café del Rey as any other couple would in a small Texas town.

The Café del Rey was packed, with many of the local high school bands cutting up and creating a scene that almost tipped toward chaos. The waitress eyed Charlie and waved him to a couple of seats left open among the high schoolers.

"Swell," remarked Charlie under his breath.

"What?" Penny rolled her eyes.

"Exactly," he agreed and squeezed her hand. She was beginning to feel familiar.

He watched her devour several hot tortillas, after plowing through her fair share of the warm homemade chips and to-die-for organic salsa. They were now waiting for the entree, the Café Special, to arrive.

Positioned in the restaurant deliberately, with thought, through experience, O'Neal quickly knew enough about every face in the café, every twitch, and every twitcher. He was happy to watch the entry doors and delighted in Penny's interests and opinions. They matched for the most part with his own. Charlie always thought of himself as a jolly good fellow, on time, neat, ready.

"You're stunning, you know, Penny," Charlie quietly shared, a little out of practice.

Penny looked up and smiled at Charlie. Her baby blue eyes sparkled, and she chuckled. "No makeup, very little sleep, in someone else's clothes and you say I'm stunning. What is wrong with you, Charlie?"

"You remembered the lip gloss."

They laughed and began to chow down the house special plates. O'Neal slid two twenty-dollar bills under his plate, then stood to scan the area. He reached out for Penny to take his hand as they sped out quietly through the parking lot to the pickup. Charlie let the dog out again and off they went to Aunt Dana's house.

The pickup jumped onto the blacktop and sped eastward to Houston in the darkness.

Penny and Charlie reverted to conversations of comfort, income taxes, abortion rights, and foreign diplomacy failure. When the subject of the 9-11 terrorist attack arose, Penny began a five-minute dissertation on the overwhelming evidence supporting the theory of an inside job. The documented squib detonations below the impacted floors, the mysterious crew of workers who entered the World Trade Center just a few weeks before 9-11, the coincidental insurance policy purchased, and together Penny and Charlie recited fact after fact, strengthening their common understanding of an epic con executed by the globalist government to perpetuate the well-being of the military complex. And suck trillions of dollars out of the system and burden it with unconscionable debt. Charlie was impressed. Penny understood the big picture.

O'Neal's pocket vibrated, and he reached to retrieve it, to find a message and five attached photos relayed from the game cameras around his house. Three men in assault gear and long guns walked onto Charlie's lawn before separating. One close-up confirmed that the men failed to don their face gaiters before passing the first camera.

Two men showed Mexican gang tattoos on their necks. The tattoos would make the men easy to identify. Both Zeta and the Sinaloa cartels were now marking their members for economic reasons. By covering their employees in facial and other highly visible tattoos, they were effectively making them *un-hirable* anywhere else, and in turn, slaves of their organization. Entire families, generations of them. Dependent and ignorant of anything beyond their next meal. We're supposed to educate them? They are like wolves.

For members of the Mexican drug cartels, the grim reaper-like image of Santa Muerta—whose winding roots can be tracked back to the Aztecs, as well as Catholicism and Voodoo. Santa Muerta is believed by some to be the Queen of the Underworld or a Saint of the Dead, and some have speculated she has a cult-like following among the pagan cartels. The belief is that by honoring Santa Muerta, the dead, the *investor* buys themselves more Earth-time even though they've committed undignified acts.

The text O'Neal sent to Darst and Demi said, "Four armed cartel goons just visited my home. Sending pics to Ryan. Close to destination."

Pulling onto his sister's street, Charlie mentioned, "Dana and I have always been there for each other, and she'll treat you like family. Just try to do a couple of things for me, please. If you must leave the house, hide yourself in the car when you leave the house and return. And please be careful when we talk on the phone. I don't want her to get too involved if possible. This is becoming extremely cumbersome with all these layers."

Penny calmly remarked, "You think?"

"Now duck down, Penny," Charlie said. "I'll let you know when it's ok."

Several minutes passed while O'Neal looked for anything out of sorts at Dana's house. When he was satisfied, he texted Dana to say, "Please unlock the door so we can sneak in?"

He walked around his pickup to Penny's door, opened it, and said, "Let's go," grabbing her hand and pulling her to the doorway and into the house.

"Hi, Charlie!" exclaimed Dana as she hugged him. "Hi, I'm Dana," she said to Penny as she extended her hand. "We're happy to have you here and you can stay as long as you need to," Dana said and winked at Charlie, escorting them to the living room. "What kind of trouble has Charlie gotten you into?" asked Dana.

Charlie was quick to answer, "Dana? Can't we relax a little before you interrogate Penny? She's had a rough couple of days. Yes, I am responsible for most of the trouble, but not all of it."

"Oh? I see." Dana sat back in the chair and waited silently. Charlie calls it the mid-western seething calm. He took a deep breath.

Charlie began to count off with abbreviated alphabet soup and a mostly sanitized version of the recent days to his sister, and her husband, Chuck, in the background, and as he was attempting to dance around some of the details, Penny noticed the baby grand piano in an adjacent room. O'Neal continued to raise his sister's level of comfort that they weren't responsible for a crime but of growing importance to the feds, but Penny remained fixated on the piano. Charlie had accepted a glass of Irish when he realized Penny had slipped into the next room and was perched on the piano bench staring down at the keys. In one, smooth motion, Penny's hands reached the keys and began to produce a flawless version of Chopin's "Piano Concerto No 1" from memory. Charlie and Dana looked at each other in total wonderment.

The piano fell silent, and Penny rose and returned to the living room only saying, "It's been a long time. Your piano is beautiful," she remarked, looking at Dana and then tilting back her glass of Cabernet.

"Wow, Penny, that was amazing!" Then she slowly pivoted toward her brother. "Ok," Dana said, turning to Charlie, "what's the deal, Charlie?"

"Wait a minute," Charlie replied. "First things first. I'd like to know how you learned to play like that?" he asked Penny. "You don't have a piano in your apartment."

Penny smiled. "I had a demanding mother who wouldn't allow me to date in high school," she said. Charlie was gob-smacked. He caught himself and turned back to Dana.

"Penny just needs not to be seen, Dana," Charlie offered. "Here's some money for anything she needs, including clothes and personal stuff. Whatever you can get delivered, please do that. If you have to go somewhere, try to sneak in and out of here, ok? Use caps, umbrellas, that kind of stuff? And, if you need to reach me, use her flip phone. Don't say anything on your phone, got it? Penny, I also need your apartment key. I will be back later, or as soon as possible.

Penny, are you ok with this? I'm sorry, but I must also leave Jolie with you."

"I guess so, there's not much of a choice, is there?" Penny wrinkled her nose.

Dana, phone in hand, sat down next to Penny and began shopping online, only looking to Charlie to say, "Shopping with other people's money? We'll see you later."

Charlie turned his attention to the television where his brother-in-law Chuck was focused intensely. A well-respected oil and gas attorney, Chuck had previous law enforcement experience, so Charlie wasn't too concerned about Penny's and Dana's safety with him around. Their son, Clark, was a deputy in the local county Sheriff's department, which added a layer of comfort to Charlie. The local Houston news channel continued to run information regarding Amanda Johnson, but no cause of death was provided. Memorial services were being planned and the African American community was preparing to make a martyr of Johnson in a big way. Congresswoman Mays had made an official statement, that Ms. Johnson's tragic death was a crushing blow to all who knew her and created a hole in everyone's heart. Johnson was lauded for her dutiful conduct and devotion to the state and country.

"What bullshit," barked O'Neal. "Hear that, Penny? As if she fell on a grenade for her comrades! Hell, she was murdered! Mays has *some* nerve. *Shitbirds*, all of them!"

Charlie drained his glass and returned to the bar in the hallway for a refill. Dana gently placed her hand on Penny's and muttered, "Don't worry, Penny. We'll be ok. Charlie and Chuck won't let anything happen to us, they just won't."

Penny couldn't stop the tears from filling her eyes, and she closed them as the exhaustion and stress took over. Amanda? Dead?

"Chuck," O'Neal said, "thank you for letting me drop this in y'all's lap. As long as Penny keeps a low profile, nobody will think to come over here and get in your business. I will create some false activity in Austin to distract these guys and make them think Penny is hanging around there. We just need to buy some time, that's all. I've got to head back home but really, I'm very grateful to you both. Stay frosty, Chuck. Hope Clark can help in watching the girls?"

Charlie and Penny eased around the corner and immediately embraced, then kissed like it was the last ever. He whispered, "I'll be back in a few days." Penny nodded, understanding, and Charlie walked out into the darkness.

"It is the rule in war, if our forces are ten to the enemy's one, to surround him; if five to one, to attack him; if twice as numerous, to divide our army into two. If equally matched, we can offer battle; if slightly inferior in numbers, we can avoid the enemy; if quite unequal in every way, we can flee from him." -Sun Tzu

Chapter 7

Overall, drug overdose deaths in the United States are rising dramatically. Methadone aside, deaths involving synthetic opioids (primarily fentanyl) continue to rise with 73,838 overdose "deaths" reported in 2022 alone, in the USA. Drug "overdoses" are immeasurable, but millions of cases are reported annually. It's estimated that nearly a third of people who abuse drugs began using pain medications temporarily for an injury. Many more are users introduced to opioids by bad actors. You know who you are. It's escalating, unwittingly ingesting fentanyl. Instant death.

Hydrocodone is a semi-synthetic opioid medication schedule II drug, approved by the U.S. Food and Drug Administration and used to treat severe chronic pain that requires opioid analgesia. It functions as an opioid receptor antagonist and activates opioid receptors to produce analgesic effects. Unfortunately, it also activates the delta-and-kappa-opioid receptors as the drug's concentration increases beyond the starting doses. No longer just a dependence, it's a dependence leading to a raging addiction. *Feed me! Little Shop of Horrors* depicts that in spades. It has to be fed.

Add ethanol (alcohol) in any form, and you have yourself a bonfire. Sue Darst, Michael Darst's wife, was a bonfire and who could intervene? In the end, God did.

Michael Darst became aware of Sue's predilection for prescriptions long before the botched dinner with the O'Neals. He knew her problem, and she knew that he knew. Everyone knew. There was anger, lots of unspoken anger just simmering, that Sue carried. Michael grew wary of her incapacity to fulfill the obligations of a CEOs' wife, and it took many months to wean her. She gradually relinquished the various duties and charitable positions to which she had committed a great deal of her life to protect her own security, his reputation, their three "issues," and the "grand-issues," of which there were several.

It became commonplace for Michael to watch Sue retire to her bed by 8 in the evening and not wake until 10 the next morning. Several of Sue's friends distanced themselves from her, while one friend who lived in a vodka bottle grew closer. Sue could reliably be found at the Country Club ladies locker room with her buddy in the afternoons testing the vodka martinis concocted at the locker room bar and grill.

Early on, Michael's overwhelming business responsibilities provided a distraction and a cure, and the answer to Sue's postpartum depression and sliding lifestyle. In the beginning, she would fly to New York to shop. That made her feel better. After a while, it wasn't enough. She flew to Milan for magnificent sweaters and to Switzerland to show the bloody things off. There was plenty of money and Michael wanted her to be happy, and to live a meaningful life. The rigors of his CEO role would drain him on most days. It took all his energy to get himself home in the dark and rummage in the refrigerator for something to eat. By then, Sue would be in bed snoring. Or off vaccinating pre-school children in hurricane-battered Haiti.

He nearly grabbed her by the throat. "You have three children of your own, it's Christmas Eve, where the hell are you? You're where? Feeding someone else's children? Sure, I can feed them breakfast cereal with heavy metals? Oh, until you get here? When? On Thursday?"

She became indifferent to Michael over time and turned instead to her drinking buddy and the pills for comfort. He developed his own resentment of Sue, mostly for her conscious and willful choice of paint remover over him and their family.

Sue's physician, whose wife also often participated in the martini laboratory, was more than happy to shovel the pain killers her way. To date, she owned 114 Louis Vuitton handbags, some originals, that she traded for 1,000,000 pills. Street value of pills $100,000. Street value of the designer handbags $350,000. He did require her to visit his office regularly to build the file justifying the meds, but Sue essentially had an unlimited supply of hydrocodone at her disposal.

Michael covertly met with Sue's physician, who gave Michael all the right responses, then proceeded to call Sue to complain that he felt somehow betrayed. Sue, of course, confronted Michael angrily in an enabled state and the communication between the two diminished to that of two unhappy roommates. Sue meanwhile repaired the relationship with her physician to return to the status quo.

The routine, albeit shifted, became a part of life for Michael and he had resigned himself to the fact that he would keep up the façade as best he could. Sue, though, continued her downward spiral. The martini potbelly and piano legs notwithstanding. The predictable conclusion to the life of Sue Darst was reached less than one year after Sophia O'Neal fell victim to the MRNA vaccine.

On that day, a drunken fifty-eight-year-old woman flopped into bed and gobbled one-too-many opioid candies. Sue's heart, already numbed by the alcohol, experienced deep bradycardia and eventually her heart simply fell asleep. She would not regain consciousness.

As on every other day, Michael entered the bedroom the evening prior to Sue's death to shower and change. He noticed her snoring and gave no thought that he would find her lifeless body the next evening, having barely moved from the evening before. He had loved Sue, and he had missed her for months. Now he found himself fighting considerable anger, that she had essentially quit the marriage and quit trying to be a better version of herself. It was several months after Sue died that he realized a few painful human realities.

People can't give you what they don't have.

People say they want you to be happy, but they don't.

Bad news never gets better with time.

If your chicks grow up and fly away, celebrate, you did a fine job!

Michael and Sue's three grown children each came donned in black and sans spouses and grandkids to Houston for the service, their oldest son from West Texas, the middle daughter from Austin, and the youngest daughter from Georgia. Respect for Michael from the "energy community" provided an industrial avalanche of superficial sympathy for the Darst family. Within the walls of the Darst home, however, Michael felt a new and uncomfortable coolness from his children. They had become strangers.

He speculated that the adult children, although mostly unaware, were less than satisfied with how he had managed Sue's habit of throwing back a handful of junk knocked back by a snifter of whiskey. *The anesthesia is what killed your mother*, he wanted to say again, like he had too many times already. I invited her to try a fancy Palm Beach rehab and she damn near burned down the house. But no one, especially Darst, was willing to bring it up now. Or ever. Whichever came last. She was gone. Nothing to see here.

It occurred to Darst that they might be here at their mother's funeral at her bequest. She would want them to do the right thing, not disappoint their father, or drink too much. They learned from their mother to keep up appearances and to play along until Mother's cash, bonds, and jewels were doled out.

Charlie and Penny became Darst's strongest supporters, exacerbating the children's frustration. Each finding their own rationale, promising to get together, the usual, but they never would. The three Darst children returned to their lives, leaving Michael to wrestle with his and Sue's demons alone.

Charlie perhaps understood Michael's struggle more than anyone, having experienced a similar tragedy when Sophia died. The two men learned to lean into each other, like brothers strengthening the bond between them. Penny's presence and contributions made everything hum.

John Milton, Michael's oldest friend, also brought Michael a strong source of assurance.

Milton and Darst had covered a great deal of everything together and could start laughing out of the blue, the two of them barely coherent holding their bellies laughing. Years of hard-fought political battles and some softly conducted reconnaissance had forged a two-headed Texas icon. There had been countless examples of one helping the other, sometimes solicited. Campfires always made Darst sentimental, which likely spurned him to say one evening on the back porch to Milton, "Do you remember when we conspired to get that King fellow elected sheriff in Montgomery County?"

Milton chuckled, "Who could forget that? That was fun, and we learned a hell-of-a lot and failed royally, didn't we? They would start laughing again. They knew too much and even laughed about that.

Over the weeks that followed, Milton managed to keep Darst somewhat productive and yet he wisely left space for Darst to grieve his loss his way. O'Neal would occasionally join Milton and Darst in the campfires, and together, the three frat boys of different eras, clinked glasses, patted each other on the back, and coasted together through the normal flashes of sorrow and loss.

Charlie covered an expansive range, from Austin to Edna to Houston and back. As he approached Austin, O'Neal pulled Penny's phone from the Faraday bag and sent texts to his own phone with a few cryptic messages.

A Faraday cage is a phenomenon that was constructed by scientist Michael Faraday in 1936. The envelopes work because an external electrical field causes the electric charges within the cage's "conducting material," which protects sensitive electronic equipment from external radio frequency interference (RFI). They block electromagnetic waves.

O'Neal used various methods to innocuously reach Penny's apartment, and once inside, sent texts to her friend at the foundation. Through an app he ordered food for a single woman. He would bag the phone and station himself near the apartment door to intercept the food delivery and eat it on the way to his office. The routine worked well until he saw two men heading up to Penny's apartment one night, loitering in the street, walking about. He stood in a tight alley lined with trash containers between brick townhouses and waited. Finally, they were ready to walk. He followed them back to their car and memorized the car's plates.

In a meeting the next day, O'Neal recounted the incident to Darst. After minutes of silent deliberation, Darst said, "We need to send a message to this bunch of hoodlums, whoever they are, that we won't be intimidated. I wish it didn't come down to this, but the consequences are just too unwieldy."

O'Neal then volunteered, "I'll take care of them. In a way that will make them pause."

Darst stared at O'Neal, then turned to stare out onto the park across from his office. "I can't tell you to do that, Charlie, at least right now I can't," said Darst. After a considerable pause, he continued, "But if you were going to do it, is there something you have in mind?"

"Fentanyl," O'Neal said. "Can we get our hands on some fentanyl?"

"I'm sure that we could, if need be," replied Darst. "What are you going to do?"

"It's one hundred times stronger than morphine. Fingerprint-less."

"Our compadres with Texas Department of Public Safety should be able to accommodate."

"Make the call," said O'Neal. "Just give me the contact info and I'll take care of it. Screw this. It needs to be gone."

Darst scribbled a name and a telephone number on a scratch pad and handed it to O'Neal, who briefly looked at it, breathed deeply, and strode out of the office knowing that he was stepping into a realm of darkness. Good men are required to occasionally do bad things for the good of those they wish to protect, O'Neal reminded himself.

O'Neal's contact was a mid-level Department of Public Safety manager, who secured the requested contraband and met O'Neal in a twenty-four-hour pancake house on Austin's south side. A solemn man, Charlie introduced himself and the two sat in a booth and began an innocent conversation about the people watching in such a place and time. O'Neal learned of his military experience, and they shared stories of their tours in the Middle East. Finally, the man retrieved an envelope from his coat pocket and slid it to O'Neal, saying, "Be careful. This stuff will kill you."

And at that, he rose, shook O'Neal's hand and offered, "Stay safe, brother."

O'Neal sat down and stared at the envelope for some time while he finished his coffee.

He pocketed the envelope after wrapping it in a napkin and headed to Penny's apartment once again, this time stopping along the way at a drug store for latex gloves and Dimethyl sulfoxide, or DMSO. DMSO is a chemical that is known for its ability to be absorbed through the skin, dissolves many organic and inorganic substances, and is available over the counter.

Carefully parking a couple of blocks from the apartment, O'Neal found a dimly lit parking place and pulled in. He pulled on two latex gloves on each hand, grabbed the envelope and DMSO, and headed for a place to conceal him while he concocted a deadly mixture of ground up fentanyl and DMSO. Falling back into a patrol mentality, he waited from a darkened corner for the car to hopefully reappear. Hours slowly passed but his patience was rewarded when the car quietly pulled into a space across from the apartment, very close to its previous location. The two men in the car talked quietly and walked directly for the apartment building's front door, where they glanced at the unmotivated security guard. It took O'Neal only seconds to sneak behind the car, enter the car, and lightly smear the mixture on the inside door handles and steering wheel.

As quickly as he approached the car, he vanished. He waited for the men, who reappeared while calling someone. Amateurs, and careless amateurs at that, he thought. They jumped in the car, started it up and drove down the street to the stop sign. The car turned left at the stop sign, and soon after it disappeared, O'Neal heard the faint sound of a metal-on-metal crash. He began walking toward the direction of the crash, and as he turned the corner, he paused and watched for any movement from his hidden position. The occupants in the rental car were motionless, the driver slumped over the steering wheel.

O'Neal traveled in the shadows and returned to Penny's apartment. He turned on a few lights, ran some water and sent a few texts. While guzzling a bottle of water, it occurred to O'Neal that it might be a good idea to peruse her emails. Opening her inbox, he was shocked to see over one hundred emails. He called Penny from his burner phone, and they reviewed the contents of her inbox together.

"Wait," Penny exclaimed. "What was that email from Maggie?"

"Says she has some mail for you in the office," O'Neal replied. "One is an envelope from Amanda Johnson. The envelope feels like there's something in it besides a letter. Penny, we better get our hands on that envelope pronto."

Penny quickly continued, "Reply to her that a friend of mine named Charlie O'Neal will be dropping by to get my mail. Say that I fell running on Caesar Chavez and will be having emergency surgery to pin a broken wrist. She's heard about you, and she won't question that."

"Do you run on Caesar Chavez? And what did you tell her about me?" O'Neal asked.

"I run there a lot," answered Penny. "All I have told her about you is that I recently met you and that I hoped I would hear from you more often."

"That's reckless, don't you think, to run on Caesar Chavez?" questioned O'Neal.

She turned and her eyes burned holes in Charlie's own. "You jest," she said.

"Fair enough," Charlie acknowledged. "I'll stay here tonight and pick up your mail in the morning. Sweet dreams, Penny."

"To you too, Charlie," Penny softly answered.

Charlie napped for a few hours on the sofa. All he could think about was the white lily on Penny's thigh and her fragrance.

The following morning, Austin was consumed in a torrential thunderstorm. Charlie constructed a small incendiary device from a household cleaner and a used milk carton. Placing his latex gloves and smearing the DMSO across the contents in the milk carton, he carried it to dumpster, lit the milk carton, and tossed it in, creating an actual dumpster fire. The Uber dropped O'Neal a short block from Congress Avenue, and he found the rest of his way to the foundation office, completely drenched.

The receptionist greeted Charlie with, "I'm sorry, sir, but I can't allow you to loiter here, in spite of the weather," as if O'Neal was one of the thousands of homelessness that plague downtown Austin.

"I'm supposed to pick up some mail for Penny Townsend," snapped O'Neal. "I'm Charlie O'Neal," he stated directly to the receptionist.

"My bad," replied the receptionist, who began searching under her desk for mail. Unable to locate the mail, she dialed Penny's assistant Maggie. The facial expression of the receptionist changed to that of relief, and she looked up at O'Neal. "Maggie will be right with you."

"Thanks," quipped O'Neal.

When Maggie appeared, her curious expression didn't impress O'Neal, who glanced at the package, thanked the assistant, and returned to the empty, storm-ravaged streets.

Jolie greeted him at the door with her usual exuberance and followed him into the kitchen. She fetched a treat, and he boiled water for tea. He showered and called Penny to discuss the contents of the package before he returned to Houston. By early afternoon,

O'Neal was again in the CEO's office. Darst began to ask O'Neal for an update, but Charlie shook his head to telegraph Darst to not inquire. The men sat in silence until O'Neal asked, "May I have a Scotch, sir?"

Darst rose without answering, "How many fingers? Two?" He remembered and brought O'Neal a glass. He stood with O'Neal, they clinked glasses, and Darst said, "Saw a headline from Austin about two Mexican Mafia thugs who were found dead in a rental car. I don't suppose you would know anything about that?"

"Can't say that I do," O'Neal shrugged and replied.

Darst raised his glass and continued, "Here's to your brave contribution for Texas, Charlie. I will never forget it."

"I wish you would, sir."

They continued discussing the current dynamics of the movement and built a short list of action items in preparation for the upcoming legislative session. As their discussion drifted, O'Neal braced himself to ask, "How are you faring?"

Darst swirled his glass, looked down into the Scotch, and answered, "Most days are ok, you know? Haven't heard from my kids, and I have learned to take care of my myself again."

"Sorry to hear that your children don't keep up with you," O'Neal responded.

"Thanks, Charlie." Darst smiled. "We'll see."

Charlie had fought his anxiousness to see Penny and it didn't take long for him to call her to check in and let her know he was on the way. Penny remarked that she missed him terribly, causing the hair on his arms to stand up, and that she and Dana had become fast friends as Charlie had expected. Turning into Dana's neighborhood, O'Neal calmed himself with square breathing techniques and he regained focus on looking for anything unusual or out of sorts as he approached his sister's house.

As he neared the house, O'Neal texted Penny to let her know he was on the front porch and about to ring the doorbell. In mere seconds, the door swung open and there stood Chuck, Dana, Penny, and Jolie.

"Quite a greeting party!" Charlie exclaimed. Jolie was excited by the commotion, rubbing up to him for a head scratch.

He crossed the threshold and closed the door just before Penny swarmed him with hugs and kisses. Chuck and Dana smiled at each other as Penny and Charlie kissed.

"If y'all would allow, I need to visit with Penny for a couple of minutes," O'Neal said to Dana and Chuck.

"Of course," Chuck replied.

"Of course." Dana nodded.

Charlie grabbed Penny by the hand and led her into a bedroom and he closed the door behind them. Penny rushed to put her arms around his neck, and Charlie allowed it if just for a few seconds. He then pulled away from her slightly and said, "Let's look at the envelope from Amanda, Penny."

She looked into Charlie's eyes and nodded.

Penny dumped the contents of the package on the bed, and a dozen or more indistinguishable envelopes were sorted until Charlie held one envelope to Penny's view. She carefully studied the envelope, and tears began to fill her large blue eyes. She tore the end of the envelope and pulled out a folded piece of paper with something taped to it.

A simple, silver locket on a chain, not unlike any to be found at a local mercado or flea market. Primitive and inexpensive. Penny turned to the note from Amanda and read it aloud. "Penny," the note read, "I saw this locket and thought of you. This is just a small thank you for your friendship—Love, AJ."

Penny stared at the locket for an eternity, when Charlie grabbed her wrist and the two stared into each other's eyes, suddenly realizing that the locket might be the vessel in which Amanda would redeem herself from the nasty, grueling work at the Mays' office and years of covering up and protecting a vile, evil politician. With the care of a diamond cutter, Penny cradled the locket just above the bed cover and paused.

Slowly, she turned the locket to its friction-clasp pin, but her short fingernails struggled to catch the pin. O'Neal instinctively produced his knife and offered it to Penny, who then easily tripped the pin. She lowered the knife to the bedcover and stared into the locket, which presented a microchip like an oyster bringing to light a magnificent pearl.

"Now what?" asked Penny.

"Now we get Ryan Becker on the phone," Charlie answered. "Would you happen to have access to any documentation explaining the disappearance of the NGO money that you think may have gotten Amanda killed?" O'Neal added, "We need it to link Mays to her death."

"There is a printed copy of the financial statement in my office," Penny shared. "And the digital download from GuideStar should be in my email. I'm sure the financials have been altered since I met with the congresswoman."

"I'm equally certain. We better get into the network at the foundation ASAP," remarked Charlie.

He called Ryan Becker and shared the situation with him. Penny saw a sense of relief in Charlie's face as he snapped the phone shut.

"Man, I can't believe how good that kid is," said Charlie. "He said he can read the chip, and he'll have the files from the foundation in a few minutes if we can get it to him."

Charlie pocketed his phone and pulled Penny close to him. After minutes of passionate kissing and holding, O'Neal called Darst with the good news and they returned to the living room and to Chuck and Dana. Lest they forget Jolie, who was dancing in a circle, impatiently waiting for some love.

The night passed rapidly as O'Neal recounted, although leaving out some minor events, the day's events to Penny, Dana, and Chuck. It became evident to O'Neal that Chuck and Dana were staunch supporters of his efforts to root out the tyranny and get the country back on track.

Charlie and Penny retreated to a darkened bedroom and devoted what night remained to pleasing each other.

O'Neal's technology lead, Ryan Becker, was quickly able to provide the renter's name of the cartel goons' car, a New Jersey corporation, and the principal of the corporation whose address was in DC. The information was passed to Darst, who reached out to John Milton. The two mulled over possible responses and outcomes, similar to the war games practiced by the U.S. Pentagon. Not surprisingly, The New Jersey corporation responsible for renting the car in Austin was a single member LLC, owned entirely by a partnership in DC.

The partnership, in turn, was constituted by an LLC whose members were BBR1 LLC, MBR12 LLC, and SBR33 LLC. The address on record was a Paterson, New Jersey address, a well-known office representing LLCs and partnerships. Most inquirers of ownership would be stymied to learn anything of substance beyond this, but Ryan Becker was not like most inquirers.

The network security system that monitors and controls incoming and outgoing network traffic is monitored for deviations. Network-based firewalls are positioned between two or more networks, typically between the local area network and wide area network, in order to observe and control the flow of data between these connected networks.

The firewall of the agent's front office network was easily penetrated by Ryan and provided an open invitation to peruse the QuickBooks software after Ryan located the password.

Payments received for services by the agent were documented in detail as the agent was always prepared for subpoenas from state courts to investigate financial crimes. Ryan combed the activity related to the multiple LLCs and the partnership, learning that all were created at the same point in time, and fees received were wires sent from one bank. The ACH information number of the bank was that of a Panama bank whose account number appeared to be occluded and replaced with a stand-in placeholder.

Ryan began to execute word searches within the files of the agent's network in New Jersey and the framework of multiple entities came into focus, to such a startling degree that Ryan feverously began downloading and printing dozens of pages to ensure the information would not be lost. Over the next hour, he learned of an intricate network of companies funneling funds to another bank and ultimately to a series of individuals' bank accounts in Panama. He eventually located telephone contact information and started to dial when he saw "Pandora Papers," which caused him to knock over his coffee cup and jump back from his desktop.

Ryan called O'Neal, and before O'Neal could inject a word, Ryan released a dosage of verbal diarrhea on his discovery of the alphabet LLCs, the Panama bank connection, and ultimately, the telephone contacts. O'Neal, visibly stunned, sat down and closed his eyes to assimilate the information.

"Are you absolutely certain?" asked O'Neal.

"Yessir, no doubt about it," replied Becker.

"And you have the documentation to prove it?" O'Neal again asked.

"I do, but I obtained it in a less-than legitimate manner," Becker answered.

"Ok." O'Neal laughed, albeit nervously. "I expect you to safekeep this intel, wipe your trail, and maintain a copy at an alternate site, understood? I will need this in my hands very soon."

"Understood," Becker replied, and he hung up the phone.

Ryan clenched his fist in victory and told his wife, "We're goin' out, tonight!"

Charlie immediately dialed up Darst.

"I have an update," O'Neal stated.

"Ok," said Darst. "Let's hear it."

As Darst listened to Charlie lay out the details, Darst interrupted, "Before you go any further, we need to get everybody together. And when can we get our hands on the financial information from Penny?"

"There is a paper file in her office and a third-party report in her work email," O'Neal answered. "I need to take her into the office to get the file. Her assistant won't be able to find it, and it's a good idea for Penny to show her face occasionally. It puts the natives at ease."

"You need to be careful here, Charlie," Darst remarked. "Let me know if you need Demi. Now, listen carefully. When you have the files in your hands, call me, say the word, and I'll set up a meeting at the ranch with the whole team. By the by, how's Penny holding up? I expect to see her. She's in their cross-hairs and she probably knows it. Can we still count on her?"

"Believe so, yes," O'Neal answered.

Darst returned to his Scotch and stared at the fading pictures of Sue and his three children.

Chapter 8

The life of Amanda Johnson was celebrated at a funeral service at Friendship Baptist Church in her hometown of Houston. The graveside ceremony that followed was held at a massive east Houston cemetery, and demonstrated a devoted following of Ms. Johnson, with loved ones from every part of her life crowding the gravesite. Family, friends, local sports celebrities, teachers, and politicians all paid homage. Among the hundreds of attendees was Amanda's boss, U.S. Congresswoman Mays, along with her new chief of staff, Li Jun Gao. Representative Mays was front and center, with all the trappings of the Queen of Sheba.

Charlie, Penny, Bill Darst, and John Milton quietly arrived ten minutes after the gravesite ceremony began, and Penny was well-disguised for the event, save and except for her five-foot, ten-inch frame. The wonderful, sleek black suit and cloche Charlie bought for Penny improved her demeanor in a big way.

Penny located Mays, who had donned a lavender pillbox hat and was sporting fire engine red lipstick, and said to Charlie, "Give me your knife and I'll stab her myself."

Charlie bit his lip to prevent erupting in laughter. This is new, he thought, deciding not to share that observation. So, this is how wood nymphs respond to stress. Interesting.

"This might be a good time to tell you my great-grandmother came over from Sicily. She believed in stabbing someone in the back twice after they're dead, then cutting them in half, and burying the two halves in separate holes in the ground, in different states, topped off with a few bags of lime," Penny shared. "You make sure they have no legs, confined to that hole. Forever."

He buried his face in the crook of his elbow, like he was about to sneeze, in order to quell the urge to laugh. Charlie couldn't quite determine if she was kidding, or what? It was hilarious, he told Darst later.

"She might be onto something," Darst said, and once again Charlie wasn't sure if he was kidding.

Demi Riojas was also present at the gravesite, watchful, heavily armed, blending into the crowd, yet within proximity to protect the team if needed. The black umbrella Charlie brought served well to minimize Penny's outline, and Charlie was of course armed, his head on a swivel.

O'Neal was not a fan of executive protection, but his training to penetrate executive protection was extensive, just a different perspective, and much more interesting. Funerals, to Charlie, were a whole other thing altogether. He abhorred funerals as they ushered in all the triggers, the memories, ugh. He knew today that the primary risk to Penny in this crowd would be within arm's length. Ever vigilant, his mind drifted to the tattoo, and her fragrance again. It had become his go-to place when he was parked in neutral, revving.

Charlie offered a handkerchief to Penny, who had her eyes closed holding back tears. He reminded himself that Penny was going through a bad piece of road, losing a friend to a c-word like Mays and turning her own life upside down, hiding out from the same evil fecal matter who was now pretending to be a mournful friend of the deceased. He would just snap her neck and be done with the nasty business.

Congresswoman Mays was never a close colleague to John Milton, and strangely so as they were both native to Houston. Mays was a prototypical third generation welfare recipient, and Milton grew up selling overpriced funeral services in May's very neighborhood to help pay his tuition and bills at Baylor University. They were taught differently their entire lives. Mays, to squeeze the system for all the juice, and Milton, to use his expanding skills of persuasion. Their very cool and formal exchange just after the graveside service had the appearance of a Kennedy-Khrushchev meeting. Mays' problem was that she didn't know what she didn't know.

Milton and Darst were inclined to extend immense compassion toward Penny. She later remarked to Charlie that it had a huge impact on her, and on how she regarded them. Michael Darst struggled with the ceremony, it being close, only a few months, to his wife Sue's passing. The stoic Marine in him took over and stifled all emotion, to anyone. That evening in his office, he numbed his pain with Scotch and eventually sobbed out loud and let it out. He implored God for answers, and not hearing any yet, picked himself up and drove to his ranch outside Gonzalez.

The odds of a tiny chip finding its way there were infinite odds. If God did not have his hand in this, creating this day from raw cloth, sending them off into battle, well-fed and strong, to fight, fight, fight… A chip. The chip. On his desk in five hours. Darst fell on his knees and sobbed for what seemed like days. And when he was done, he was reborn. Right there. He was certain that everything that had occurred in his life was meant to be. The last time Michael Darst heard buzzing like this he was examined for vertigo. His jaw relaxed for the first time in years. He surrendered that day, and everything in his life changed. The world changed. By a chip and the Almighty.

The first microchip was invented in 1974, and today they are the brains of every electronic device in existence, from watches, to calculators, to satellites, to computers. A microchip is an integrated circuit etched onto a silicon chip, or wafer, and serves to transfer electric currents or signals to a receiving device. With wires and transistors, it creates a highly conducive environment for transferring electricity. Co-invented in the late 1950s by Jack Kilby from Texas Instruments and James Noyce from Fairchild Semiconductor—the integrated circuit is a vast improvement from the vacuum tube and transistor—it doesn't burn itself up and it plays well with other components, like connecting a cell phone to the Internet or connecting to live or video conferences. These miracle bits keep track of activities and information—such as the voice messages Congresswoman Mays would leave, or send, and stacks of printed documents and hundreds of email threads. Moreover, in televisions, GPS tracking devices, and identification cards, always collecting random bits of flotsam, data, and secrets. Microchips don't discriminate; they send accurate destination addresses within seconds, making information available, and sometimes too available, as in dangerous.

Penny's recently killed friend Amanda moved many documents. The microchip in the locket was brilliant and a loving parting gift; Amanda knew the risks. What she provided was a vivid, compelling portrayal of Congresswoman Mays, and not in a good way. The documentation of the representative's dealings with contacts in Washington, DC, the NGO Our Lady of Perpetual Light, in Del Rio, Governor Harper, and so much more was damning. If a heap of documents was not enough, there were audio recordings of Mays' instructions to Amanda and telephone conversations containing explicit details of children being shuttled from the Del Rio facility to Dallas, Chicago, New York, and DC in a manner that would resemble a cattle trader. Like Christmas gifts boxed up and mailed to distant friends, the nameless children were passed around as enviable gifts.

Becker, who retrieved the materials, was overwhelmed by the enormity of the trafficking. O'Neal, after speaking with Becker, was forced to drop everything and visit him to check on his emotional well-being. Protocols prevented the information from transmitting digitally through the team, and O'Neal needed the thumb drive of the hot material to be safeguarded. A brief visit was indeed the appropriate step. Not one to be wasteful, O'Neal picked up Penny in Houston that night and the couple drove to Austin. The first challenge was to sneak Penny into her apartment for fresh clothes.

O'Neal stopped at an outdoor store in Bastrop and picked up two pounds of Tannerite to create a diversion. Tannerite is a brand of binary explosive used for firearms practice and "baby bombs." The targets comprise a combination of oxidizers and fuel, primarily aluminum powder. The combination is relatively stable when subjected to forces less severe than a high-velocity bullet. Rarely triggered by electricity, and its fire retardant, it can ignite everything around it. The store O'Neal chose to patronize was old school, loved cash customers, and asked no questions.

Sold as separate components, which are not themselves explosive, Tannerite is not regulated. Duct tape, a single round, and a few springs were enough to convince the entire neighborhood that a gang was shooting up the place two blocks from Penny's apartment. The trash pickup service did its part by arriving on time, and when the garbage truck driver dropped the dumpster back onto the pavement, the Tannerite did its part, creating an explosion that echoed for blocks. The driver bailed out of the truck onto the asphalt, afraid for his life, in need of another pair of underwear and a couple of paid days.

"All warfare is based on deception. Hence, when able to attack, we must seem unable; when using our forces, we must seem inactive; when we are near,
we must make the enemy believe we are far away; when far away,
we must make him believe we are near."
Sun Tzu

The haphazard security in Penny's apartment building, now absent due to the nearby explosion, gave Charlie and Penny the chance they needed to grab suitcases of Penny's clothes and personal items and waltz away undetected. As they rounded a corner to the awaiting Uber, Penny suddenly dropped her bags to the ground.

Charlie wheeled around, and Penny put her hands on her hips and said, "This is enough! When are you going to let me be part of this insane movement, Charlie? You drag me around, squeeze me for information, seduce me, and sometimes you even talk to me like I'm this fragile butterfly."

"Wood nymph," he corrected her.

"What?"

"I've seen it."

"Oh," she said.

"You're already in." Charlie paused, then said with a grin, "Hell, Penny, I thought you knew that you were in. And it's a fine bunch of reprobates we are."

"Whose truck are we taking?"

"Please get in the car?"

The Uber pulled up that would take them westward to Congress Avenue. Penny asked Charlie, "Can I have a gun?"

"You know how to shoot, do you?" Charlie asked.

"How hard can it be?" Penny remarked.

O'Neal grew close to Penny's face and said, "We sneak around some cartel thugs, you watch me blow up some shite, and that makes you a tough girl?"

"I can take care of myself."

"See this face? This is me laughing out loud, Penny," he said, turning her around. "I just don't want you to get hurt. These Mexican mafia dudes may not be sophisticated, but they are ruthless. And they will burn you in oil after they torture you. Please let me take care of you. I promise I'll teach you to shoot, ok? Now, may I remind you that we should be blocks away from here by now?" O'Neal insisted.

Penny grabbed her bags and got into the back seat of the Uber, with Charlie right behind. Eventually, Charlie looked at Penny, whose eyes were streaming with tears. She leaned over and put her head on his shoulder, sighing deeply. O'Neal stopped the Uber at a hotel for a few hours' rest.

The last hundred yards to Charlie's truck was undertaken on foot. The two, having the appearance of awkward tourists, loaded the suitcases and bags of Penny's clothes inside O'Neal's pickup truck and walked to a nearby coffee shop. Ever watchful, O'Neal bluntly requested an open booth in the corner, a vantage point. Charlie pointed Penny into the corner seat facing the restaurant and he slid in beside her.

Her puzzled look spurned Charlie to explain, "It's just so that I can see the place without any surprises."

"Do I have to sit next to you?" Penny asked.

O'Neal nodded and grinned.

"I'd like to talk about how we'll enter your office this morning," Charlie began. "We'll stop by a drug store to pick up an arm sling and some sport wrap to put on your arm. Decide now what your injury is and keep it simple. Introduce me as a friend or someone visiting from out-of-town, whichever you're most comfortable with.

Use my first name only, ok?" Penny listened intently as O'Neal continued coaching her on small details of body language and tips to help keep the visit short. Charlie saw something amiss with Penny, and he stopped.

"I'm sorry for the role I played in turning your life upside down," Charlie said, leaning into Penny. "We have been granted a place at the banquet, and being on the inside is overwhelming if you over think it. Giving Texas back her sovereignty, well, what can I say? But there's a big price we'll pay as well. If you really want to be involved, people are going to find out, you might lose your job, and you will be called all kinds of crazy things, a crackpot, lunatic, traitor, and probably much worse. History shows it happens, so expect it. You'll probably lose friends and maybe even some family."

Penny stirred her cup of coffee and cream, pondered the laminated menu, and replied, "Whose car are we taking?"

A grin came across Charlie's face, a grin that Sophia would have caused, a grin that a grown man rarely gets to share. That moment ushered in a new era of their relationship, a partnership with a common vision of determination and perseverance.

Penny showed her coolness and personal strength as she updated her co-workers with the improvised story of her fall, while never really losing the momentum to get into her office and out. Charlie was introduced to several colleagues as a close friend from Houston that, "I met at a fundraiser." Charlie maintained his quiet but friendly tenor, nodding his head *hello* as the coworkers gradually drifted out of her office, leaving Charlie, Penny, and her assistant to talk privately.

"I'm fine," Penny told her assistant, who looked at Penny incredulously.

"If you say so," she remarked. "Your hair looks different, maybe a comb? And you never come in here dressed like you're heading to a swap meet. But if *you* say so."

Penny reviewed the incoming material on her desk then turned to unlock her file cabinet and fingered through several files, occasionally tossing a file on her desk. The small stack of files was placed in a Trader Joe's shopping bag and while Penny offered a few parting directions to her assistant, Charlie checked the hallway and waved to her "all clear" and they were gone. *Poof.*

Once Penny and Charlie reached the side street which led to his truck, Penny looked at Charlie and asked in stride, "So how did I do in there, Charlie?"

"You were marvelous, Penny," Charlie remarked. "You'll make a top-notch spy in no time."

O'Neal chose a different route away from the office out of caution, and they carried the bag of documents into a copying center in a nearby strip center. Two copies were made of all the documents, and a set was scanned and put on thumb drives. One set was boxed and mailed to Michael Darst and one set was mailed to Charlie's office. With originals in the bag and thumb drives in Charlie's pocket, they returned to Charlie's pickup, where Charlie texted Darst that everything went as expected.

"How about you give me a reader's digest condensed version of all these files?" Charlie requested.

Penny smiled and said, "The information contains financials directly from Our Lady of Perpetual Light, the trail showing the missing funds, and the banks used to transfer the funds. Another file has the history of the children who came to the facility over the last few years and who eventually left and where they initially went. The paperwork that accompanies the children and documents with their ultimate disposition are also there. And there's more, but I get so mad at Congresswoman Mays when I think about all this, I can't seem to focus."

"That's understandable, Penny," Charlie said. "It's hard to keep your perspective when you are neck-deep in it. I'll try to help you with that, but for now just close your eyes and breathe."

As Charlie and Penny sped down Highway 290 toward Giddings, Charlie's phone rang. Darst asked Charlie to bring him up to speed, and Charlie said, "It would be better coming from Penny."

Penny reluctantly took the phone and gave Darst a thorough review of the documentation. Darst asked her some questions, which she answered in perfect detail. She said goodbye and handed the phone back to Charlie.

Darst instructed O'Neal, "Charlie, does Demi know to show up this evening?

"Not sure, sir, but I can give him a call," O'Neal replied.

"Please do so," Darst continued. "And ask him to come early and to give me a call when he's fifteen minutes out."

"Understood," O'Neal confirmed. "Everything ok? Anything else?"

"Everything is good. Tell him to pack for six days," Darst replied.

"Yessir, will do," said O'Neal.

Lt. Governor West received the important news of the events relating to Our Lady of Perpetual Light and Congresswoman Mays the day after the funeral for Mays' right arm staffer. His telephone conversation with Milton was brief but intense, both men realizing the moment was approaching. Quick agreement was reached that a meeting of the team was immediately necessary, and the instructions were distributed. West, Milton, O'Neal, Townsend, and Darst would gather that very evening at Darst's ranch and the remaining leaders would arrive the next day.

By mid-afternoon, West, Milton and Darst were deep into the particulars, in the sanctity of the den in the "Big House." Darst paced like an expectant father, waiting for the chip to arrive. The others, drawing lines and delineating districts, agreed that it must be five o'clock someplace in the world, say Bombay. Scotch was on the table and crackers and spread were nearby.

The Guadalupe River bordering the Darst ranch provided small barge travel to deliver the cotton crop to San Antonio Bay on the Gulf of Mexico in the nineteenth century. On the eastern side of San Antonio Bay was the small port town of Seadrift, where ocean-going vessels took on cargo for delivery to the east coast. The "Big House" was painstakingly returned to near-original form, thanks to Michael and Sue Darst. Twelve-foot-high ceilings, beautiful long-leaf pine floors, and an endless number of double-hung windows created an atmosphere like Tara in *Gone with the Wind.*

The house library doubled as a den, with several overstuffed easy chairs and a hand-carved billiard table in the room's center. Notepads and coffee cups occupied every horizontal surface, and the three men deliberated many courses of action related to the extraordinary information in their possession. It was a rarity when emotion became a part of the dialogue. Darst and the Lt. Governor were clear in their deference to Congressman John Milton, senior to both in both age and experience.

Once the chain of events was recounted in detail, Lt. Governor West stood up and walked to a window. He looked out through the pecan grove in silence, and Milton and Darst continued their discussion without West's participation.

Milton finally raised the question, "Are we boring you, David?"

West spun around and replied, "Sorry, John. It's Penny Townsend. I've known her for a long time, and years ago we had a brief thing, before I was married. It ended as quickly as it started, and I believe we are still on good terms. Just wanted to be transparent with y'all."

"Well, there's a wrinkle for you," Milton quipped. "No love child out there somewhere, is there? Anyone else aware of this tryst?"

"Not to my knowledge," West replied.

"Michael, it's pretty obvious that Charlie O'Neal is smitten with this girl, and I suppose we need your best guess if you think this could be a problem," Milton asked.

Michael Darst pondered the question. He lifted his chin slightly and scratched his throat with his hand. "Unlike me, John, Charlie doesn't look back. He is completely focused on the here and now. This effort we've undertaken is the most important thing in Charlie O'Neal's life, I promise you. If their relationship continues, or grows, I still wouldn't bet against Charlie for one second."

"Fair enough, Michael," Milton stated. "But you might consider informing Charlie of this little tidbit just in case she has told someone. Your call. David, please call Penny's boss at the foundation and insist that she take on an assignment reporting to you, which will require her to work remotely for two or three months. Tell him it will be worth it to the foundation, eventually. We've got to keep her safe."

West nodded positively. Darst nodded and turned a stern glance to West, but Milton swiftly brought them back to the larger looming challenges.

"David, why don't you give Michael and me a *no* BS assessment of the house reps in Austin, who's with us and who are on the fence? Names, numbers, the whole enchilada," Milton suggested.

"Sure, John. A good place to start I think is with the folks on the fence. Out of the eighty-five Republicans, there are approximately twenty that could go either way, and on the Democrat side, maybe another fifteen to twenty. Call it a total of thirty-five to be safe. The easiest bunch to count is the naysayers, and there's easily thirty Democrats and believe it or not, probably forty Republicans."

After a long pause, Milton asked, "How is Manny doing in getting them to lean our way? And how long will it take for Manny to give us a breakdown and a list? And, given the bomb we're about to drop on the governor, what will be the fallout?"

"Manny is, of course, the best there is, and he continues to have wins. I think the work he will be sharing with the group will speak for itself. It's just tough, John, you know that, and now we're shortening the runway. Governor Harper, well, he's not without enemies, and I suspect he'll find himself alone on a desert island once the news hits. And it couldn't happen to a nicer guy," West added.

"Remind me what the protocol is when the governor misbehaves like this?" Darst asked.

Milton raised his hand to stop West and said, "Good question, Michael, but the group needs to hear this as well. David can provide the chain of events from his perspective, and we'll let Laci offer her perspective as well. There may be others caught up in this damn mess, and we should be ready."

Demi Riojas, always the soldier, was ready in minutes to leave for Gonzales. His gear was remarkably robust for one civilian. Night optical devices, or NODs, fully integrated with two 5.56 mm rifles, handguns, cans of ammunition, spotting scopes, camouflage netting, remote video cameras, cases of bottled water, radios, all tools of the modern-day warfighter. As he approached Darst's ranch, he called Darst as instructed. Darst fully instructed him of his role and the accommodations set aside for him during his stay. Demi would provide for the safety and well-being of the nucleus of the soon-to-be Republic of Texas leadership, with the help of Charlie O'Neal. Demi was pumped in anticipation.

The group members began streaming onto the ranch the following morning, with everyone present by ten o'clock in the morning. Just weeks earlier at Milton's ranch, the general tenor was relaxed and optimistic. But not now. There was a seriousness, an intensity crackling in the air.

Milton allowed everyone to settle in, and as the group found their way to the dining room, which served as a makeshift conference room, a sense of hopeful optimism welled up within him. The mahogany table and chairs in the room's center were beautifully matched by armoires at each end of the room. A single Texas flag stood in one corner, fringed in gold. There used to be an American flag that stood beside it also edged in gold fringe. The United States of America Corporation. Sue was determined to cut that into pieces when Robinson was elected, but she was raised by staunch conservatives and the thought of defacing a flag was like heresy. Darst took it down and stored it in the garage. That was that.

Before him was this group of highly talented and motivated patriots, all willing to put personal agendas aside to help breathe life into the dream of liberty for Texans.

Milton began by saying, "Charlie is going to cover some housekeeping, then we'll move to the business that brings us all here. Charlie?"

"Thanks, everyone," O'Neal began. "Remember, all iPhones should already be in faraday bags and cannot be used for the duration of the meetings. Once you are more than an hour away from the ranch, you can check your phones and email again. Also, please welcome Penny Townsend." Charlie extended his hand toward Penny. "Penny's help thus far has been critical, and she has endured a great deal in a small amount of time. Her friend, Amanda, as some of you know, lost her life, probably, to the cabal, including Mays. Penny has shown toughness, courage, and quick thinking. Her role moving forward is still being finalized." Lt. Governor West looked out of a window.

Milton thanked Charlie and said, "It is appropriate for us to remain mindful of those brave souls that pledged their lives, their fortunes, and their sacred honor almost two hundred and fifty years ago in Philadelphia.

"The prayer I'm about to read was adapted from George Washington's Circular Letter to the States, which he wrote on June eighth, seventeen eighty-three as Commander-in-Chief, at his headquarters in Newburgh, New York. I have taken the liberty to amend only two words, which you will surely notice."

I now make it my earnest prayer, that God would have Texas in his holy protection, that he would incline the hearts of the Citizens to cultivate a spirit of subordination and obedience to Government, to entertain a brotherly affection and love for one another, for their fellow citizens of Texas at large, and particularly for their brethren who have served in the field, and finally that he would most graciously be please to dispose us all, to do Justice, to love mercy, and to demean ourselves with that Charity, humility and pacific temper of mind, which were the Characteristics of the Devine Author of our blessed Religion, and without a humble imitation of whose example in these things, we can never hope to be a happy Nation. Amen?

"Amen," was the refrain in unison.

"Michael, would you kindly lead us in the Texas *Pledge of Allegiance*?

"I would be delighted."

Michael Darst rose, and everyone around the table pushed their chairs back to stand and placed their right hands over their hearts and began as one, "***Honor the Texas flag; I pledge allegiance to thee, Texas, one state under God, one and indivisible.***"

Milton resumed, "Hopefully, your accommodations will suffice for the next few days. If you need anything, please let me know. The computer in the study has access to the internet for unrelated browsing and news. Make yourselves at home. There is so much for us to wrestle with, yet so much talent with which to work. It isn't my desire to commandeer this agenda, although there are some minimum requirements that we should all agree on in principle. Everyone here has a unique set of skills, and the importance of the situation demands that we all feel empowered to freely voice our opinions. We will employ Robert's rules of order and nominate and approve an officer to lead this session only. Are we in agreement so far?"

Everyone nodded in agreement, which made Milton chuckle.

"So far, so good. Remember these things, please," he continued. "In my estimation, we must discuss and agree in principle on term limits, balanced budgets, treaties, our share of the U.S. debt, defense, the constitution, civil service, and taxation. There certainly may be other matters important enough to obtain our attention. We'll see if we can hash through all of these. In place of a secretary at this juncture, I have made available a stand-alone digital recorder activated when we sat down. Everyone is welcome to review the discussions, but no editing will be done. That said, is there a motion to nominate a presiding official?"

"I nominate Michael Darst," volunteered O'Neal.

"I second the nomination," said Manny.

The pause that followed said it all.

"Hearing no other nominations, Michael Darst it is," exclaimed Milton.

Darst stood and took control of the meeting, opening with a brief statement.

"This is not a role that I sought or desired, but since y'all chose this, I'll do my best," Darst remarked. "Now down to business, the chair opens the floor for discussion as the group sees fit."

"Perhaps we should discuss possible committee structures to tackle the many items John mentioned earlier," Laci suggested.

"I agree," said Elena. "With such a small group, we can each lead a committee and serve on a couple more, to put three people at a minimum on each committee."

Ideas were floated across the table to provide structure and expectations of the various committees for several minutes when Michael interrupted.

"Let's take a five-minute break and we'll dig in," Darst said.

Penny spared no time getting near enough to Charlie to say, "There's something you need to know."

Charlie looked into her eyes, giving her his complete attention. "Ok, let's have it."

"Lieutenant Governor West and I have a history," Penny confessed contritely.

Charlie scratched his cheek as the blood drained from his face. "Ok." He breathed deeply. "Is there more?"

Trying quickly to regain his color and composure, waiting for Penny to respond, made Penny freeze, slack-jawed, not knowing what to say. From the dining room, they were called back into the meetings before more could be said.

"OK, ok, everyone, let's move on," Darst called, to quell the chatter. "I will take the budget and taxation; Elena, please take treaties; Laci, the constitution; John, the US debt; Manny, Term Limits, EEOC, Insider Trading and Congressional Ethics. What's left? Oh, yeah, Charlie, defense, to include immigration. That should keep us busy. The first meetings will be the constitution under Laci and the US debt under John. Stay conceptual if the issues become too complex, ok? If major points can be quickly hammered out, do so. Build the scaffolding of our new and improved 'Republic of Texas, the Greatest Country in the World' frameworks, ok? We'll plan to reconvene in three hours."

Effortlessly, the group divided into hubs and one group remained in the dining room. The others made their way to the study and began serious debate on likely necessary amendments to the Texas constitution which soon led to term limits discussion and mandatory civil service or military service.

Darst, O'Neal, Townsend, and Attorney Laci excused themselves and retreated to the master bedroom, where Darst locked the door behind them with a brass skeleton key.

"What's up?" Charlie asked him.

Darst raised his eyebrows, like Dudley Whiplash, and circled his hand above his head. "It's a saferoom."

Now, Charlie raised *his* eyebrows. He looked around. "Wow."

Everyone had eyes on Charlie, almost panting, as he took the locket out of the inside pocket of his sports coat. He handed the locket to Penny, who held it up with a great smile.

"Come on now..." drawled Darst.

"Ok, hold your horses while I pry this thing open." The clasp clicked, the dented heart opened, and there she was. "All babies are beautiful," Darst said softly, as if not to wake it. "Come to Papa, you beautiful thing. We're going to make you famous, darlin'."

They locked her away and all of the documents, for now, in a gun safe and resumed the business of designing the Republic.

"The current state Constitution of Texas was adopted on February fifteenth, eighteen seventy-six, and is the seventh constitution in Texas history. The previous six were adopted accordingly in eighteen twenty-seven while Texas was still part of Mexico and half of the state of Coahuila y Tejas; eighteen thirty-six was the Constitution of the Republic of Texas; eighteen forty-five upon admission to the United States; eighteen sixty-one at the beginning of the American Civil War; eighteen sixty-six, the end of the American Civil War; and eighteen sixty-nine," Milton read to the group. Lest they forget.

"We will preserve the wisdom of our forefathers while embracing global opportunities and romancing constraints," he continued. "Our values portray who we are. I stand with the Lord and the Ten Commandments. I will fight for the right to be a free man, and if someone thinks they can just jump the fence and tell me I can't, well, I'm packing the Second Amendment right here in this pocket. Come and get it. We Texans, we got soul, we got grit, and we got country. Like I said, 'Come and get it. Make my day.'"

They cheered. Penny even had tears in her eyes. Charlie was on the other side of the room, leaving Penny to fend for herself. Everyone stood to pledge the Texas Flag and when they sat again, Penny was not in the room. And Charlie, who can eat hot chilies without an issue, felt suddenly sick to his stomach, the news about Lt. Gov. West threw him for a loop. He knew he couldn't change history. He'd tried.

Darst assigned O'Neal to look through the house for anything that could be used as a weapon, besides cutlery in the kitchen. That was obvious. Darst returned to Milton's lecture in the dining room. "The documents from earlier times were pieces of art. Take a look for yourselves. Micheal here has several exquisite copies under glass hanging in the foyer. But more important than the esthetics is the content, of course," he continued eloquently, and Darst pulled up a chair.

"The document explicitly provides for the separation of powers and incorporates its Bill of Rights directly into the text of the Constitution as Article One. The Texas Bill of Rights is considerably lengthier and more detailed than the federal Bill of Rights and includes some provisions not included in the federal Constitution. A significant difference is Section Twelve which recognizes the writ of Habeas Corpus as a right and prohibits its suspension under any circumstance. This differs slightly from the

U.S. Constitution, which allows its suspension 'In Cases of Rebellion or Invasion the public security shall require it.'

"Section Twenty-One prohibits corruption of blood and forfeiture of estates, including in cases of suicide, extending beyond the federal limitation in Article Three, Section Three, which applies only in cases of treason and even permits forfeiture during the life of the attained.

"Section Thirty-Four guarantees the right to hunt, fish, and harvest wildlife, subject to wildlife conservation laws. However, the section explicitly states that it does not affect 'Any provision of law relating to trespass, property rights or eminent domain.'

"Section Thirty-Two, added in 2005, denies state recognition of same-sex marriage, a practice invalidated by the US Supreme Court ruling in *Obergefell v. Hodges*.

"Section Four purports to prohibit officeholders from the requirements of any religious test, provided they 'Acknowledge the existence of a Supreme Being.'

"Section Thirty-Nine allows a bill to take effect immediately upon the governor's signature if the bill passes both chambers by a two-thirds vote unless otherwise specified in the bill. If the bill does not pass by this majority it takes effect on the first day of the next fiscal year, which in Texas runs from September first until August thirty-first.

"Section Forty-Nine A requires the Texas Comptroller of Public Accounts to certify the amount of available cash on hand and anticipated revenues for the next biennium; no appropriation may exceed this amount except in cases of emergency, and then only with a four-fifths vote of both chambers, and the comptroller is required to reject and return to the legislature any appropriation in violation of this requirement.

"Critical to the Texan group's discussion is Section Sixteen of this article, where the lieutenant governor automatically assumes the power of governor *if and when* the governor travels outside of the state or is subject to impeachment by the Texas House of Representatives.

"A consideration of the group at the Darst ranch was mandatory national service, or compulsory service, as a requirement that people serve in the military or complete other works of service. Modern propositions for compulsory service envision that young Texans could join the military or do civilian projects such as teaching in low-income areas, helping care for the elderly, or maintaining infrastructure, roads, and highways, among other ideas.

"Proposals in the United States to implement compulsory service traces back to the eighteen hundreds. More recently, between two thousand three and twenty thirteen, former US Representative Charles Rangel from New York made five unsucccssful attempts to pass the Universal National Service Act, which would have required all people in the United States between ages eighteen and forty-two to either serve in the military or perform civilian service related to national defense. The US military draft, created during the Civil War, is one type of mandatory national service. However, although all male US citizens ages eighteen to twenty-five must register with the Selective Service, the United States has an all-volunteer army and hasn't drafted men into the military since nineteen seventy-three when around two point two million men were drafted into the military during the Vietnam War.

"Public opinion on mandatory national service is split, with forty-nine percent favoring one year of required service for young Americans in a twenty seventeen poll, while forty-five percent are opposed. Not surprisingly, among adults ages eighteen to twenty-nine, who would be required to complete the service, thirty-nine percent are in favor of the proposal and fifty-seven percent are against it. The committee agreed to table the notion for now.

"The idea of legislative term limits predates the Constitution. In a two thousand nine research paper, political scientist John David Rausch Jr. documented the long debate over legislative term limits back to the time of the Articles of Confederation, which held that 'no person shall be capable of being a delegate for more than three years in any term of six years.' James Madison's Virginia Plan, introduced at the Constitutional Convention in Philadelphia in seventeen eighty-seven called for legislators "to be incapable of reelection . . . after the expiration of their term of service, and to be subject to recall."

Rausch pointed to several theories about why the founders ignored Madison and excluded term limits from the Constitution. One theory was the practice of voluntary rotation of office already observed in state legislatures; another was that the delegates could not agree on the length of service; and another was that the states were empowered to determine the limits of service for their members of Congress.

Madison's *Federalist No. 53* warned that tenured representatives could thoroughly become the "Masters of the public business, and perhaps not unwilling to avail themselves of those advantages." But an inexperienced legislative body would be "more apt to fall into the snares that may be laid for them." (Note: The National Archives attributes authorship of *Federalist Nos. 53 and 62* to James Madison.)

The idea of term limits for the presidency gained traction during the 1940s, in light of President Franklin D. Roosevelt's four terms in office leading to the ratification of the 22nd Amendment in 1951, which limited a president's time in office to two terms. However, the debate over term limits for Congress did not peak until the mid-1990s.

During the 1990s, a key Supreme Court decision shut down one proposed path to term limits in Congress: Action taken by the states to place their qualifications on their members of the senate and house. Arkansas changed its constitution to block candidates from the ballot for the House of Representatives if a person was elected to three or more terms, or the U.S. Senate if the person was elected to two or more terms. Another twenty-one states had taken similar measures.

In *U.S. Term Limits v. Thornton*, a divided Supreme Court ruled that states could not add qualifications for office for members of Congress in addition to those explicitly stated in the Constitution. Writing for a five-four majority, Justice John Paul Stevens said that "the Framers decided that the qualifications for service in the Congress of the United States be fixed in the Constitution and be uniform throughout the Nation." There was only one way to change the qualifications. "In the absence of a properly passed constitutional amendment, allowing individual States to craft their qualifications for Congress would thus erode the structure envisioned by the Framers," he concluded.

Justice Clarence Thomas wrote for the dissent: "Nothing in the Constitution deprives the people of each State of the power to prescribe eligibility requirements for the candidates who seek to represent them in Congress. The Constitution is simply silent on this question. And where the Constitution is silent, it raises no bar to action by the States or the people." However, since the Court's decision in 1995, it is understood that only a constitutional amendment could place term limits on members of Congress. The group gathered outside. Gonzales understood well that a constitutional amendment would afford the legal underpinning to the legitimate concerns of professional politicians.

Attorney Laci James, Manny, David West and Penny Townsend produced a draft constitutional amendment to ensure term limits for all elected officials and additional guidelines for the elimination of any government employee or entire department who was appointed or traditionally hired. The debate centered chiefly on achieving competency over all else.

Penny initially provided meaningful service with her extraordinary typing skills. As the discussion progressed, however, her intuitive ability to build consensus and soften opinions was noticed by the more senior members. In fact, during the first break of the afternoon, Lt. Governor West and Manny pulled Milton aside to share their newfound respect for Penny Townsend, and they went on to say they were convinced she should lead the meetings with Democrat reps who were not staunchly opposed to their cause. Penny, they remarked, was innately effective at keeping an issue from being dismissed or decided prematurely. Milton studied West to discern an ulterior motive, but Manny's insistence of Penny's talents gave Milton confidence. Penny, meanwhile, tried to do damage control with Charlie during the break. Charlie was tepid toward Penny, but not cold, and Penny forced herself to stay focused on the work of the group, freshly reminded of Amanda and her murder.

Milton, Garcia, Becker, and O'Neal began their discussions of the U.S. debt in a conceptual manner, and eventually reached a consensus that the inheritance of the state's proportion of U.S. federal debt could be discussed congruently with a discussion of a balanced budget. With the U.S. interest payment on its debt reaching historic levels, the difficult and contentious issue of money, as in any divorce, was sure to be hotly debated.

In a 1997 essay by David Blum entitled *The Apportionment of Public Debt and Assets During State Secession* published in the *Case Western Reserve Journal of International Law,* Blum noted that:

"Extended bargaining over the apportionment of the public debt and assets could prove costly because cool-headed calculations may not be easily made during heated secession negotiations. A heated debate between the seceding state and the parent state over the apportionment of the public debt and assets could affect both states' international credibility rating. Additional activities hurt by a prolonged debate include future trade between the two states and the states' participation in financial markets. A quick agreement between the seceding state and the parent state on the apportionment of debt and assets is imperative to a smooth, peaceful, and inexpensive transition to independence."

Daniel Miller, founder of the Texas Nationalist Movement, stated in his hallmark work, TEXIT: "*It has been customary throughout the world that, when a state secedes from a larger country or confederation, it voluntarily accepts a position of the national debt. This was the case with Singapore leaving Malaysia in 1965 and Bangladesh when it left Pakistan in 1971.*"

The 1983 Vienna Convention on Succession of State in Respect of State Property established that a seceding state had an obligation to assume a portion of the debt in any superseding agreement between the two parties.

Four different methods were identified by Blum in his 1997 essay. A per capita approach simply divides the total U.S. debt divided by the total population, then multiplying that dollar amount by the population of Texas. Another approach uses GDP which takes Texas' percentage of overall GDP as a percentage of the national debt to be assumed. The third is a Historical Benefits Approach, where the amount of money paid into the federal system by the State is compared to the amount of money that has been paid by the federal system into the State. This ratio is applied as a percentage of the national debt and is the amount owed. Last, the method Blum refers to as the Historical Tax Shares Approach which uses a balance sheet method to match federal assets with liabilities.

Each federal asset is valued and allocated to a portion of the debt incurred. Therefore, the debt service payment is the same percentage as the assets received. Texas would assume a dollar of debt for each dollar of assets. If the assets apportioned to Texas are greater or less than the amount of debt apportioned, the amount of debt to be assumed by Texas is raised or lowered to equalize Texas' share of the public debt and assets. Most difficult and tedious, and subject to the interpretation of current value and absence of accountability by the federal government, this approach would be the last method of choice by both parties of interest.

Balanced budget amendments are defended with arguments that they reduce deficit spending and constrain politicians from making irresponsible short-term spending decisions when they are in office. Research shows that balanced budget amendments lead to greater fiscal discipline. However, there is substantial agreement among economists that *strict annual* balanced budget amendments have harmful near-term economic effects. In times of recession, deficit spending has significant benefits, whereas spending cuts aggravate and lengthen recessions. To prevent that, most balanced-budget provisions make exceptions for times of war, national emergency, or recession, or allow the legislature to suspend the rule by a supermajority vote.

Poland's constitution adopted in 1997 caps the public debt at 60% of GDP—the government cannot take on any financial obligations that would cause that limit to be exceeded. To ensure this level is never breached, Poland has a self-imposed debt threshold of 55% of GDP, and the government must take action to balance the budget once this level is exceeded. The *Articles of Confederation* and the *Perpetual Union* had granted to the Continental Congress the power to borrow money or emit bills on the credit of the United States, transmitting every half-year to the respective States an account of the sums of money so borrowed or emitted and, with this as a model, Article I, Section 8, Clause 2 of the Constitution grants to the United States Congress the power to borrow money on the credit of the United States. When the Constitution came about, the United States had a significant debt, primarily associated with the Revolutionary War. There were differences within and between the major political coalitions over the possible liquidation or increase of this debt.

As early as 1798, Thomas Jefferson wrote, "I wish it were possible to obtain a single amendment to our Constitution. I would be willing to depend on that alone for the reduction of the administration of our government; I mean an additional article taking from the Federal Government the power of borrowing. I now deny their power to make paper money or anything else a legal tender. I know that to pay all proper expenses within the year would, in the case of war, be hard on us. But not so hard as ten wars instead of one. For wars could be reduced in that proportion; besides that, the State governments would be free to lend their credit in borrowing quotas."

The issue of the federal debt was next addressed by the Constitution within Section 4 of the Fourteenth Amendment (proposed on June 13, 1866, and ratified on July 9, 1868):

The validity of the public debt of the United States, authorized by law, including debts incurred for payment of pensions and bounties for services in suppressing insurrection or rebellion, shall not be questioned. But neither the United States nor any State shall assume or pay any debt or obligation incurred in aid of insurrection or rebellion against the United States, or any claim for the loss or emancipation of any slave; all such debts, obligation, and claims shall be held illegal and void.

One of the earliest Balanced Budget Amendment proposals presented in Congress was that of Senator Millard Tydings, who introduced Senate Joint Resolution 36, a resolution in support of a Constitutional Amendment that would have taken away some of the flexibility the U.S. Treasury had accrued concerning debt management by proposing to prohibit appropriations above revenues in the absence of a new debt authorization and require that any new debt be liquidated over fifteen years.

Steve Forbes, the American publishing executive and former presidential candidate proposed a flat tax plan in 1996 and advocated keeping the first $33,000 of income exempt. Coupled with a serious reduction in wasteful spending, this flat tax could revive the economy for decades. The concept of an optional flat tax rate was developed by Forbes to address criticisms that it would eliminate popular tax breaks. Forbes' flat tax recommendations were adopted by the group at Darst's ranch, with few changes.

A rhythm was developing in the sessions, where a committee's participants would alter slightly in its composition. Elena Garcia, David West, and John Milton were fluidly moving between groups while Penny Townsend, Ryan Becker, and Charlie O'Neal remained with their small groups through several sessions. Whiteboards were filled, erased, and covered up again, and laptops were passed around tables for review.

An amount of fatigue was seen by Darst among some of his group and he ended the work sessions earlier than planned. He shared the dinner plans with everyone and declared a two-hour break. Most participants stayed in conversation and found their way to the bar for a glass of wine.

The evening meal that day was served outside on the back patio with a perfectly delivered offering of grilled quail on risotto with broccolini, followed by pecan pie.

Later that evening, Charlie took the opportunity to approach Penny. Of course, he wanted to dismiss what he had learned earlier about her and West. It would take time, though. Penny was relieved when Charlie walked up to her and struck up a casual conversation. She wanted one chance to find her way back to Charlie and the relationship they'd enjoyed before Charlie learned of her close friendship with the Lt. Governor years ago. *Just keep talking to me, Charlie,* she thought.

Chapter 9

O'Neal briefly wrestled with Penny's past but set it aside to focus on the all-important events directly in front of him. It was termed the "three-meter range" in the special operations community, focused on challenges or threats close enough to trump any potential problem farther out. Penny didn't have the luxury of the training and discipline Charlie leaned on, and her face reflected her internal struggle. As any mature person would do, she talked to herself, offering reassurance that she was making the resistance much larger than it was. She would buck up and keep on—*things work themselves out*, she told herself.

Laci James well understood that no situation in her life would ever approach the importance of this moment in time. James had built a career that any attorney in Texas would and does covet, and among the most effective tools in her toolbox was her skill in hiding her level of genius. Her husband, a talented CFO, was not fully aware of the critical nature of the situation. James and her husband had, however, developed a code with which they would communicate in vague terms throughout this most unorthodox setting. It was no surprise to him when she had covertly shared that she would be out of pocket for the immediate future but that all was headed in a good direction.

Milton and Darst had spent the late hours of the first day comparing notes on the situation and the people bringing their expertise to bear. Frameworks shaping the necessary amendments to the Texas Constitution had progressed more rapidly than they expected. Neither Milton nor Darst were concerned about the budgetary requirements of the embryonic republic. The apportionment of the US debt was a nasty and complicated matter. As in any divorce, the emotion and intensity of money are eclipsed only by the custody of the children. It was best to delay the discussion of this issue until the group became more tenured and cohesive. Emerging in stature among the tiny band was Laci James and dimming in relative importance was Elena Garcia. Tomorrow's agenda, the two agreed, should be focused on a subject that held relatively simple solutions. Treaties would be the hot topic after the legislative body strategy was complete.

The dining table was layered with stacks representing the one hundred fifty house seats in the Texas legislature. In each stack was a profile of the representative, a synopsis of the representative's district, voting history, alliances, donor lists, and a summary of contacts and conversations Manny Elizondo conducted with comments.

Milton poured through a handful of the sets to his satisfaction and nodded to Manny his approval. The next scheduled enclave would begin in a half hour and Manny, fully prepared, chugged down his glass of iced tea. He approached Milton and explained that the piles were also more or less situated on the table geographically, with the panhandle districts upper left as one looked at the table. The piles were tabbed with a red, blue, or yellow sticker further identifying the candidate by Manny's estimation of the representative's stance on secession.

"All right, everyone," began Darst, "Manny will lead this session and provide instructions. Manny, the floor is yours, sir."

"Thank you, Michael," started Manny. "This mess before you will make sense in a few minutes, but my goal was to allow us to quickly focus on those legislators that first, are on the fence, and second, are currently opposed but might be convinced through horse trading to vote our way. The file tagged with yellow is in my estimation undecided. If you will, pick up a stack in an area close to you geographically in the state. Within the stack, you'll find everything you need to know about that rep and his or her learning. Also, you will see the issues important to the rep and their voting history."

The files were browsed intensely by the group and occasionally a snarky comment arose from a group member that would in turn create a chorus of laughter. Milton and Darst carefully studied the group. The progress made and the speed at which it occurred was impressive, yet he knew that the yellow-tagged files in the group's hands were the most critical obstacle to the success of their movement.

"Once you've reviewed the file, please find the one-page fact sheet in the stack. The fact sheet is a tool to use when with the rep in person. It lays out the rationale for our secession in tangible terms to the representative. As an example, the rep in Killeen has a major concern about Ft. Hood and the consequences of a negative outcome. Information supporting our movement for the rep is attached, which educates the rep about our lease agreements with the U.S. government and agencies that will prevent a disruption to the business as usual within her district. She will also benefit directly from the stabilization of her constituents when the military population has the option to become Texas citizens. *And*, the future taxation related to her district will stay in Texas and be more efficiently directed back to her district for infrastructure, schools, etc. Just one example.

"If you think about the rep and his or her own needs, the fact sheet will give every rep at least one solid reason, and probably more, to lean our way," Manny stated. "But this is very important," he continued, "We need to be thoughtful about who we put in the room with the rep to pitch the story."

"Folks," Milton interrupted, "it's not easy, but simple. If we can garner enough of these reps on the fence and get a vote…" Milton looked at Lt. Governor West. "…then it will go our way. If we can't get enough of them to vote *aye*, we are simply preparing ground for the future."

Darst responded, "Manny, tell us more if you can, about these representatives individually, would you? Specifically, are there legislators in these stacks that carry influence within their ranks other than Jim Martin?"

Elizondo responded, "I'll think about that more, but off the top of my head, I know that reps Cesar Ramirez of Brownsville and Cynthia Vasquez of McAllen are influencers of the other reps from South Texas. Both are significantly less liberal than any of their Democratic colleagues, and Vasquez has whispered to me that she is getting a lot of pushbacks from her constituents on the illegals that are *screwing up the neighborhoods* and taking jobs. The people there are *pissed*."

"Good," replied Darst. "Any others that come to mind?"

"Not that I can think of," answered Manny.

"Ok," said Darst, "Let's get these stacks sorted, and then we'll work through each one."

James reached for the files of representatives from the Rio Grande Valley, tucked them under her arm, and walked to an armchair to review. The group wasted no time picking up a share of the other files and sat down to review them individually and build notes on the strategy. The subsequent discussion of each rep proved extremely valuable in elevating all the group members in their persuasive abilities and knowledge of the legislator. The supportive data on the district, its population, per capita income and important industries, aided in focusing their talking points and hot-button points. James allowed the others to offer their reports of the files reviewed before she asked Darst for her opportunity to share her thoughts on representatives from the Valley. From thin air, James constructed a thoughtful strategy to gain the representatives' concurrence and a means by which the rep would feel compelled to lean on their two colleagues in the neighboring districts.

Charlie was fascinated by the tactical expertise Manny showed, and he eagerly poured through stacks of legislators from Hallettsville to Corpus Christi, learning the issues critical to each representative. He began to see that most of the Democrat reps voted along party lines and a large share of the Republican reps voted according to the best interest of the local industry. He also noticed Elena Garcia was quick to defend a few of the more tenured Hispanic legislators, regardless of their posture on issues. Milton also noticed.

Over several hours, options were provided to structure the contact approach and who would make their case in meetings.

Thirty-five yellow-tagged files, lawmakers across Texas, Beaumont to Pampa, with dissimilar needs and constituents. Many times, conflicting needs among the constituents, and often a politician whose vote could be turned and justified if the quid pro quo was meaningful enough. Never in Texas had a talented and driven group like this been handed a project so important. The three women around the table, Laci James, Elena Garcia and Penny Townsend would later learn their roles would be pivotal. Penny Townsend's career was about to launch into the headlines of all major news outlets. The day was spent in tireless discussion of each representative and specific issues defining the representative. The work was grueling but thorough and resulted in clear tactics to systematically reach, meet with, and persuade over fifty legislators in a blitz-like fashion in the weeks ahead.

Almost without exception, the team selected for the critical task of convincing twenty-five to thirty representatives to re-think their understanding of Texas' sovereignty consisted of Manny Elizondo, Laci James, and Penny Townsend. After the day's meetings, the back patio of the Darst Big House offered a retreat for the team with beer, wine, and cocktails precluding the evening meal, and venison and scalloped potatoes hosted from the immense kitchen.

Collegiality among the group was on the upswing that evening. Michael appeared much more at ease, cajoling and mixing with everyone. The mood was cheerful and relaxed. Cabernet fueled

Penny's courage to intimately reconnect with Charlie and she eventually found the opportunity to lean in closely to whisper, "I miss you." He saw her eyes well up and attributed it to the second or third glass of wine.

Charlie responded lowly, "Me too, Penny. I'm still watching over you." She smiled and caught a tear before it broke.

It failed to occur to Penny that even though Charlie hadn't spoken much to her over the past two days, he was nearby. After all, far is a perception. As she studied Charlie more, she could just barely make out the slight bulging of his handgun on his waist, hiding underneath a loose and untucked Hawaiian shirt. He had been protecting her all along. She suddenly felt embarrassed that her emotions had been so self-centered.

As often happens in social settings, Penny and Laci tended to get together as girls in a boys' world, to talk about the little things that bring girls comfort, like fine threads, baubles, and boys. Penny was thrilled that she had, through fate, found a strong and accomplished woman to relate to as a peer who lived nearby in Austin. In those brief intervals between carrying out the business at hand, the two women enjoyed conversations that sometimes eased the intensity of the hour, and sometimes grew their understanding of each other, like two girls discovering a new best friend at summer camp.

Lee Hemingway intermingled with Laci and Penny in a manner that a big sister would. Hemingway was from a generation earlier and was unafraid to close in on the two younger women to comment on their shoes or hair. Always supportive and gentle, Hemingway saw the path ahead far clearer than did Penny or Laci, and it was fraught with many hidden landmines.

Elena Garcia was not so fortunate. Both Laci and Penny held an intuitive level of mistrust for Garcia. Garcia was also a generation older than both Laci and Penny, and Garcia’s demeanor seemed to possess no humor or playfulness. She was downright mean as if she had been robbed of joy somewhere in her past and wasn't giving it up to “nobody.” Laci was savvy enough to extend her hand to Elena, but always ensured herself an avenue for retreat since the dialogue tended to be little more than perfunctory. A love for Texas provided the common thread, for which they would all work.

The matter of treaties was tackled effectively. Hemingway showed a deep understanding of treaty negotiations. Her references to generally accepted treaty construction and protocols guided the team’s conversation. The governor’s recent trade agreements were reviewed and folded into the standing treaties already enjoyed by the U.S. and its neighbors Mexico and Canada. Concerning Mexico, multiple treaties exist with the United States to specifically address extradition, taxes, and water. The most famous, The Treaty of Guadalupe Hidalgo, was signed by the United States and Mexico on February 2, 1848, ending the Mexican War (1846-48) and extending the boundaries of the United States by over 525,000 square miles.

In addition to establishing the Rio Grande as the border between the two countries, the territory acquired by the U.S. included the states of Texas, California, Nevada, Utah, most of New Mexico and Arizona, and parts of Colorado and Wyoming. In exchange, Mexico received fifteen million dollars in compensation for the territory and the U.S. to assume claims from private citizens of these areas against the Mexican government. Similar treaty drafts were outlined for critical trade partners, including Taiwan, Argentina, Australia, and Germany.

As the group at the Gonzalez ranch entered the final stages of policy formation, John Milton ramped up his discussions with Lt. Governor West. Milton and Darst knew West was the weakest link in the top leadership as a politician. Politicians, as they well understood, would always be inclined to see which way the wind blows. Milton intended to be the wind that steered West.

In the study, late that evening, Milton, West, James, and Darst privately met to specifically discuss their contacts at the Department of Justice (DOJ) that would faithfully investigate and then prosecute the cabal including Governor Harper, Congresswoman Mays, and President Robinson.

As they debated the Criminal Division of the U.S. Department of Justice, as to who develops, enforces, and supervises the application of all federal criminal laws except those specifically assigned to other divisions, they understood that the enormity of the child trafficking and massive embezzlement would dwarf any scandal in the history of the United States.

United States attorneys are part of the U.S. Department of Justice and serve as the chief federal law enforcement officers in each of the ninety-four U.S. federal judicial districts. Each U.S. attorney serves as the United States' chief federal criminal prosecutor in their judicial district and represents the U.S. federal government in civil litigation in federal and state courts. U.S. attorneys must be nominated by the president and confirmed by the Senate, after which they serve four-year terms.

U.S. Attorney's Offices are staffed mainly by assistant U.S. attorneys (AUSA). Often colloquially called "federal prosecutors," assistant U.S. attorneys are government lawyers who act as prosecutors in federal criminal trials and as the United States federal government's lawyers in civil litigation in which the United States is a party. In carrying out their duties as prosecutors, AUSAs have the authority to investigate persons, issue subpoenas, file formal criminal charges, plea bargain with defendants, and grant immunity to witnesses and accused criminals.

The Criminal Division and the ninety-three U.S. Attorneys have the responsibility for overseeing criminal matters as well as certain civil litigation. Criminal Division attorneys prosecute many nationally significant cases. In addition to its direct litigation responsibilities, the division formulates and implements criminal enforcement policy and provides advice and assistance on criminal matters. Unfortunately, the Criminal Division advises the Attorney General, Congress, the Office of Management and Budget, and the *White House* on matters of criminal law.

The Racketeer Influenced and Corrupt Organizations (RICO) Act provides extended criminal penalties and a civil cause of action for acts performed as part of an ongoing criminal organization. Milton and James reached agreement quickly that RICO laws had been violated and that a senior level DOJ official, hopefully within the West Texas region, should be identified that would insist on an earnest investigation.

Under RICO, a person who has committed "at least two acts of racketeering activity" drawn from a list of thirty-five crimes (twenty-seven federal crimes and eight state crimes) within ten years can be charged with racketeering if such acts are related in one of four specified ways to an "enterprise." There must be one of four specified relationships between the defendant(s) and the enterprise. Either the defendant(s) invested the proceeds of the pattern of racketeering activity into the enterprise, acquired or maintained an interest in, or control of the enterprise through the pattern of racketeering activity, conducted or participated in the affairs of the enterprise *through* the pattern of racketeering activity, or conspired to do one of the above.

During the 1980s and the 1990s, federal prosecutors used the law to bring charges against several Mafia figures in the best-known RICO case. In 1985, United States Attorney Rudy Giuliani (who would be indicted under Georgia RICO laws in August 2023) indicted eleven organized crime figures in *United States v. Anthony Salerno, et al*, also known as the Mafia Commission Trial. Using the RICO Act, Giuliani charged the heads of New York's so-called "Five Families" with extortion, labor racketeering, and murder for hire.

James reminded everyone that, ironically, the DOJ's anti-trafficking efforts included well-intended but wasteful investigations, training, enforcement, and outreach initiatives to strengthen anti-trafficking partnerships, prevention efforts, capacity-building programs designed to advance survivor-centered anti-trafficking strategies, and granted funding to state, local, and to non-governmental organizations (NGOs). It was concluded that the DOJ likely funded Our Lady of Perpetual Light in Del Rio.

As midnight passed, the names of various DOJ contacts were tossed about and rejected. In terms of relationships, Milton easily had the strongest Rolodex. His years on Capitol Hill provided several names at various levels within the DOJ to be considered. James shared that a law school friend who had taken a position with the North Texas Region of the U.S. Attorneys was a viable contact for information. Milton finally tabled the discussion and suggested

West, Darst, and Ms. James sleep on it and reconvene the following evening.

Final sessions focused on fine-tuning policies on defense and preservation of individual liberty. O'Neal directed a meeting of Milton, Garcia, and Becker outlining the requirements to rebuild the border wall that had begun under the previous administration and abandoned by the Robinson administration. Customs and Border Patrol would be replaced by the Texas Guard and existing encampments would be remodeled. The U.S. government was operating massive facilities near border crossings to facilitate the mass importation and processing of illegal aliens, all of whom would be criminal trespassers under existing Texas law. Encampments at Ft. Bliss, Eagle Pass, and Donna required modification and major deferred maintenance.

O'Neal provided a thorough understanding of logistical and personnel requirements to accomplish border security and detention in less than ninety minutes. Darst audited O'Neal's presentation, and his confidence in O'Neal was reinforced. Elena occasionally scribbled notes but raised no concerns or questions. She was beginning to irritate some at the table.

Ryan Becker frequently interacted with O'Neal from the perspective of technology's role in managing the scarce data associated with illegal immigrants. Unmanned Aerial Vehicles (UAVs), or drones, played a critical role in the rugged terrain of much of the border. Cartels had leveraged the capabilities of drones for years to outmaneuver U.S. Border Patrol forces and redirect coyotes and their parties.

Large defense contractor lobbyists had experienced success in forcing U.S. departments to accept overly complicated and expensive platforms and systems. As it goes, *When the only tool you have is a hammer, every problem becomes a nail.* O'Neal eagerly anticipated an environment that would allow competent technicians to request systems more applicable and effective to the task.

The temporary encampments planned were spartan-like but safe. Buses would deliver the illegals to Mexican crossings several times per day, and it was anticipated that the swift actions would dramatically reduce incoming trespasses. Separately, illegals captured with unrelated children and/or drugs would find themselves deposited in a prison farm with rapid legal proceedings to formal sentencing and deportation. At this point in the discussion, Becker bolstered the plans with additional technological tools. Elena never raised her head but wrote furiously. O'Neal glanced at Darst who nodded back.

Darst resisted the feeling that the time was growing near for the group to be dismissed and that they would return to the world that held the power to keep radical movements like theirs under their boot. He felt compelled to bring the group together one final time to review their courses of action and clarify the procedures for communications moving ahead.

Darst reminded himself that some members were not privileged to be formally trained in communications. Assurance was given that the group members would not be in a vacuum alone, and partners and backups were designated. A secure digital network had been established by Becker that would prove very difficult to penetrate, allowing real-time communication and information sharing.

As the final sessions were completed, Milton, West, James, and Darst quietly met to review the steps to be taken and their final thoughts on DOJ prosecutors. John Milton had condensed a short list of officials who quietly sought guidance. The law school classmate James had mentioned the night before would also be considered.

Of Milton's contacts in the U.S. Attorney's Office, Sam Tippetts in Ft. Worth offered the best course of action, down to the actual litigator's name. The Federal Court, which was likely to hear the charges, was benched by an appointee of the previous administration. John Milton knew the judge only casually, from fundraisers and charity events. The judge, Beverly Compton, had a reputation for toughness and abhorrence for crimes and corruption.

Meanwhile, Penny had quickly become a protégé of Charlie and a source of constant questioning. Charlie was surprised by her raw intelligence and understanding of the big picture. In just days,

Charlie led Penny, now a hungry student, through the essence of boot camp and even some more advanced psychological training during the early mornings and after dinner each evening. Penny proved to be extraordinarily fit and athletic. She rapidly acquired the complex concepts of psychological manipulation, situational awareness, and mastery of small arms, thanks in part to Demi Riojas' passion and excellence with firearms.

Charlie enjoyed the refresher in pistol marksmanship, a perishable skill requiring frequent sharpening. Penny continually prodded Charlie to obtain a handgun, and in a few days, he agreed to hand over one of his Glocks. As she reached out to accept the handgun, her eyes lit up like a child being handed a new puppy. She lunged at Charlie to wrap her arms around his neck which brought a long-lost sensation of warmth and affection to O'Neal. She began to ramble about having holsters to match her outfit when Charlie put his hand up to stop her.

Charlie had closely observed Penny for many days now, and he became confident that Penny could not only handle herself well in a pinch but now had become an integral part of a movement that was becoming more dangerous by the day. Now that she had completed rigorous training, he could finally relax and allow her to become more self-reliant. That was in everyone's interest.

Elena Garcia spent the early mornings in solitude walking around the big house with her rosary beads. She was a devout

Roman Catholic of another era whose childhood centered around the church and nearby convent. Throughout her primary school education, the church's elementary school was her second home. The church gave Elena love and discipline, elements both absent in her home in San Antonio. Elena was the second child of four born to first generation immigrants from Chihuahua, Mexico. Her mother passed away one year after the youngest Garcia child was born.

Although a young girl, Elena was expected to be a primary caregiver to her younger sister. Their modest two-bedroom house was only half a block from St. Benedict Catholic Church on the west side. Elena was at the church whenever she could, depending on her responsibilities at home, preferring the sisters' friendship to other girls in the neighborhood. As she entered high school, her maturity and seriousness vaulted her to the top of her classmates and her pathway to the University of Texas was assured through parish support.

Life in Austin as a college student elevated Elana again. Volunteering at a local Catholic Church and a homeless shelter, her lengthy prior experience in parenting and serving others caused her to gravitate toward environments that cried out for help. She contemplated pursuing a master's degree in social work, but a nun discouraged her. *Aim higher,* the nun advised.

In the 1960s, Mexican American student activists at the University of Texas at Austin agitated for the creation of an academic program that reflected their lives, their experiences, and their way of knowing. In 1970, UT created the Center for Mexican American Studies (CMAS), with Américo Paredes named its first director.

Over the past fifty years, UT had become an important scholarly center for Mexican American, and Latino Studies. Once a small center borne of struggle, the center, a research institute, and a department now offered bachelor's and doctoral degrees. Elena eagerly joined the center as a freshman and remained active, serving in a leadership position through her post-graduate studies. Sometimes her ideas were new and fresh, or arrogant and radical. She grew iron-fisted and caused some colleagues to avoid her.

The Department of Mexican American and Latina/o Studies (MALS) is a group of faculty members whose teaching and research are innovative in areas of study including immigration, borders, policing, race, language, gender, sexuality, class, public health, culture, and more. The interdisciplinary faculty earn fellowships from the American Council of Learned Societies and the School for Advanced Research, win grants from the National Science Foundation and the National Institutes of Health, run labs for conducting the most cutting-edge social scientific research, and use their expertise to serve their local community. MALS faculty provides students with a rigorous education and prepares them to be smart, ethical, and politically minded contributors.

Garcia's career took her to the League of United Latin American Citizens (LULAC), specifically LULAC Council 60 in Houston, one of the oldest LULAC councils in the United States. The mission of LULAC Council 60 is to advance the educational, economic, and civil rights of Hispanic Americans through advocacy, community service, and cultural programs to promote social justice and equality. Elena's politics moved dramatically to the right during the years that Elena dedicated to the Hispanic cause, which she witnessed, expected to participate in, the blind adherence to left-wing ideology. The grifting became too much for Elena to endure and she accepted the role of Executive Director of the Hispanic Republicans of Texas, an Austin organization founded in 2009 to help elect Hispanic Republican State Representatives. Garcia experienced a wonderful sense of purpose in promoting the electability of conservative Hispanics. Her interactions with several candidates, which grew into relationships, elevated the candidate's likeability and grew their viability as a strong candidate.

In time, Elena's entire being was centered on helping others, leaving little time for family and even less for friends. She had seen more than enough of the stereotypical Hispanic male growing up in west San Antonio who had no interest in a chauvinistic woman *who should be seen, not heard, barefoot and pregnant, clean-the-house* relationship. Besides, she thought, she ran metaphorical rings around all the male Hispanics in her small circle of lucidity and problem-solving. The boys were painfully slow to mature, it seemed. Now, Elena seized the opportunity to be a part of this historical movement, to represent her race, and to ensure that Latinos would have a hand in the new republic's formation. As with all the group, Elena knew God had brought her to this place.

Milton and Darst envisioned Garcia as the conduit through which the Republic of Texas would relate with Mexico, as Ambassador. Her reputation was impeccable, and her intolerance for corruption would precede her in meetings with Mexican leaders immediately ahead. A final meeting between Garcia, Milton, and Darst nailed down the critical issues, those of immigration, the border, the cartels, and trade. Garcia was provisioned with multiple economic scenarios to share with her Mexican counterparts to provide assurances that their new neighbor to the north would provide a seamless continuation of the trade.

A final gathering of the new leaders in the makeshift conference room held a sense of nervousness, like a team meeting before a championship game. Gone were the relaxed mannerisms and conversation. John Milton intentionally fanned the flames. He cleared his throat and began, "I would like to commence by offering some words from President Theodore Roosevelt in a speech where he once said, and I quote,

"It is not the critic who counts; not the man who points out how the strong man stumbles, or where the doer of deeds could have done them better. The credit belongs to the man who is

actually in the arena, whose face is marred by dust and sweat and blood; who strives valiantly; who errs, who comes up short again and again, because there is no effort without error and shortcoming; but who does strive to do the deeds; who knows great enthusiasms, the great devotions; who spends himself in a worthy cause; who knows, in the end, the triumph of high achievement, and who at the worst, if he fails, at least fails while daring greatly, so that his place shall never be with those cold and timid souls who know neither victory nor defeat."

Milton continued, "The seriousness of our work cannot be overemphasized, and we must, of course, ask our Father in Heaven to lead and guide us. Immediately, the quiet work to win over the legislators must begin."

As the ten Texans slowly filed out of the Big House, handshakes and hugs among all the team offered visual reinforcement of their commitment to the historic cause.

Returning to Austin that day, David West removed his phone from the Faraday bag as he approached Bastrop. More than one hundred emails and many voice messages convinced him to find a quiet place to make a first pass through all the communications. He had some explaining to do to several people expecting his response. Among the voice messages were two from Governor Harper. West checked his calendar for the next few days and didn't see the governor. He listened to the voice messages, both innocuous. He texted the governor to ask him to call at his convenience and took a deep breath. Straight away the governor rang him up.

"Good afternoon, Governor," West started. "How is everything with you, sir?"

"Everything is peachy, David," the governor answered. His tone was off. "I tried calling you a couple of days ago. Where are you? Are you ok?"

"Yessir," West replied. "Just on a brief restful two days. Sorry to miss your call. Can I help you with anything?"

"No, it all worked itself out," responded the governor.

"I'll be back in my office first thing tomorrow," mentioned David.

"Ok, just swing by my office," Harper *advised.*

"Yessir, will do. Thanks," said West. He wiped his forehead and turned up the a/c in his car. He noticed his hands were shaking. This was the first time David West feared assassination, and he felt ill. He drove on, called his wife, and told her how much he missed her. "Are you ok?" she asked.

"No," he answered.

"Honey, what's wrong?"

"Just eager to be home," he said. He was having an anxiety attack, pulled off the highway, and, sat in his car for a while until it passed.

Texas State Representative James Martin, of Tyler, was first elected in 1968 at the age of twenty-five and was the longest-serving legislator in the history of the Texas House of Representatives, and the longest-serving incumbent state legislator in the United States. In November 2023, Martin announced he would run for reelection to a record *twenty-ninth* term in the 2024 Texas House of Representatives election. While a doctoral student at Baylor University, Martin decided to run for the legislature to succeed the incumbent Republican Thomas Calhoun of Tyler, who was not seeking a third two-year term. The prevailing axiom was that "Texas is run by Democrats." Although this part of Texas had been trending Republican at the national level, Democrats continued to hold most local and state offices well into the 1980s.

Martin was one of eight Republicans in the chamber at that time. His victory came on the same day that Richard M. Nixon was elected as U.S. President. In 1975, Martin was named chairman of the House Natural Resources Committee, the first Republican to have chaired a Texas legislative committee in more than a century. In Texas, a legislator need not be in the majority party to chair a committee. James and Tina Martin both had ownership interests in hundreds of oil and gas leases in the state, with a value of over $50 million.

Martin received royalties of more than $2 million per year for brokering extraction lease sales, which of course are potential conflicts of interest as he sits on the committee that oversees the state's oil industry. Martin introduced a bill that would preserve the interests of holders of overriding royalties such as his own; he had even reintroduced it after it was vetoed by Governor Harper. His history of confrontation with Governor Harper was legendary, the stuff of which gangster movies are made.

Manny Elizondo knew James Martin well. Manny had crossed the threshold of Martin's office dozens of times over the years, sometimes purely out of respect, and sometimes to seek Martin's guidance on a legislator or a specific issue. Martin was indeed the Godfather of Texas politics. If he wanted a bill to reach the floor for a vote, it somehow would. Manny also knew that Martin was wary of Manny's recent effort to sway lawmakers on secession. His reasons were logical. He had much at stake personally. If ever a state representative benefitted by maintaining the status quo, it was James Martin.

Manny, Laci, and Penny conferred at length on their approach to Martin, whose blessing would catapult their effort forward. Manny was convinced that Martin could be brought to their side if he reached a comfort level that his personal fortune was not at risk, and if the bargain had a sweetener.

Lieutenant Governor West bore stripes on his back from Representative Martin. West learned the hard way that Martin's influence and power was not to be underestimated. In the previous session, West was expected to promote a bill that, on its surface, seemed difficult to oppose.

The term performance credit mechanism (PCM) was a policy recently approved by the Public Utility Commission and opposed by groups such as the Sierra Club. The Sierra Club deemed the policy risky and expensive, putting more tax dollars into the coffers of polluting power generation companies in exchange for an untested promise that fossil fuels would not fail. Martin knew Texans mostly supported the oil and gas industry and he delegated a handful of eager legislators from the Permian Basin to develop and execute a campaign to ensure the policy would die in committee.

Lt. Governor West was not made aware of Martin's plan and mistakenly stepped out in public to garner support for the policy. Fortunately for West, the headlines running at the time involved corruption of the first family in D.C. Cocaine discovered in the White House was the gossip and intrigue the American public loved to follow. West learned from his misstep and moving forward, would always check the pulse of the Tyler lawmaker before stepping in front of a camera.

West allowed Martin a "legislative win" on occasion and the two mended fences. West, after discussion with Manny Elizondo, reached out to Martin personally to request a meeting to initially share the plans of secession in a manner that would minimize Martin's political risk. For Martin, the opportunity would be floated that he (Martin) be the presumptive candidate for a cabinet post collectively over the interior, energy, and transportation. It was common knowledge that Martin was nearing retirement from public service, and this offered a meaningful exit ramp. In exchange, Martin would pull six or more representatives to support the secession movement.

Martin had experienced the narcotic "high" of political power for more than twenty-five years. Elizondo and West understood Martin expected to be approached by West alone, not dragging along a lobbyist. But Penny Townsend, she might add a positive spin to the conversation at hand. Martin knew *of* Penny Townsend and her work with the foundation. Her policy drafts and white papers had benefited Martin's career.

Milton and West called Penny to outline the planned meeting and Penny's role. Penny thought, *What would Charlie tell me to do? Know your enemy...*

Penny engaged in the process of research that defined her as a policy analyst. Who was Martin's wife Tina? Their children? Her interests? Her family? Where did she go to school? What were her favorite clothes? Before the sun reached her window in the morning hours, Penny knew more about Tina Martin than almost anyone.

The Martins were active members of the First Baptist Church of Tyler. Tina Martin attended Vassar College for a year before getting overly disgusted with the peculiarities of the female students from the northeast. She returned to Texas and finished her art history degree at Baylor. She favored Pink Frost lipstick and preferred Burberry-labeled outfits. The causes Tina promoted were Daughters of the American Revolution (DAR) and PEO Sisterhood. Penny searched for PEO members within her circle and queried them on Mrs. Martin. She remembered Charlie's sister Dana proudly displaying DAR recognition in her home and she reached out to Dana to see if she knew Tina Martin. Penny was rewarded. Dana had met Tina at a mixer at the Petroleum Club in Houston and a friend of Dana, Jane Hanson, was in Tina's posse, which is her closest circle of friends.

Dana volunteered to set up a three-way call with Jane that afternoon. Dana further shared that Tina worked hard to be highly visible in the DAR regional leadership. Tina and James Martin had two adult children, both men who worked in the oil and gas industry. Their three grandchildren belonged to the younger son, James, Jr. After a brief call with Dana and Jane, Penny was satisfied to a certain extent that she had collected an ample amount of intel on Tina Martin and prepared a C/V (Curriculum Vitae) for dissemination to Manny, David, Laci, and John on Mrs. Tina *(nee* Stover) Martin, forty-nine.

David West sketched out the proposed cabinet position for James Martin and ran it by Milton and Darst. With only minor tweaks, the agreed-upon cabinet position West stared at appeared indeed to be compelling and prestigious.

West, Milton, and Townsend met again by phone that evening. Manny had assembled the talking points, and their roles were rehearsed and edited. Penny hung up and called Charlie to gain some reassurance that she would perform as everyone, especially Charlie, expected. Penny asked Charlie several questions about the upcoming meeting, about Representative Martin's possible responses, and how she should react. Once again, Charlie provided the balm to soothe Penny's anxiety, a special quality that he possessed and brought to their relationship. Now, she could relax somewhat and get some rest.

As Milton, David, and Penny met in the parking lot near Martin's office the next morning, Representative Martin was completing his usual morning routine. Staff had been briefed, calendars for the next twenty-four hours were confirmed, and his Merrill Lynch broker had called him from Dallas to provide an update. His option contracts on Brent Crude and natural gas were accruing value nicely. All was Monday morning business as usual.

The meeting on Martin's calendar scheduled for 10:30 a.m. with Milton, West, and Townsend was a bit of a mystery to Martin, but none of the three posed a risk to his lofty position. The mystery was centered around their motive. *Out of nowhere, the Republican Lieutenant Governor, a U.S. Congressman, and a think tank analyst wanted thirty minutes of his time...to what end?*

Self-preservation was Martin's primary motive according to David Wests' best thinking. West understood Martin needed that comfort early in the meeting, and that there was no downside to the proposition about to be laid at his feet. Penny would serve to mesmerize Martin by her ability to resemble Martin's wife Tina in ways that were purely subliminal. The clothes, the lipstick, even her scent would affect Martin's sensory system and artfully coax the conversation along, measuring Martin's receptivity and level of agreement by his words, mannerisms, and body language. It was David West who would use his mastery of the English language to convince Martin of the "bird nest on the ground." The remainder of the group held its collective breath while the trio entered the building. All this just to obtain a referendum.

The office of the senior legislator from Tyler was appropriately located and adorned. The paneled reception area adjacent to his office flaunted the recognition received by Martin for his accomplishments as a lawmaker for more than two decades. Awards and plaques adorned every wall between photographs of Boy Scouts and world leaders. A miniature oil derrick crowned the tiny coffee table in the corner, nestled between two chairs. It was simple; Martin was not.

Penny thought of her prior interactions with James Martin and the information she'd provided over the recent sessions that gave Martin the appearance of a subject matter expert. Martin really knew very little apart from the material that the foundation, most notably Miss Penny Townsend, provided, and he was spoon-fed. Martin and Penny would maintain the illusion this day, preserving his image of statesmanship. Penny understood that her role was entirely supportive. Her seductive presence in appearance and in the careful turn of a phrase, would lower his resistance to any issue that he found uncomfortable. Pure psyops. Charlie would say, "Is that an oxymoron?"

As David West carefully laid out the case for this opportunity, Penny would play a supportive role, at some juncture reminding Martin of his years of service and contributions to the state. Martin, of course, would see through the veiled flattery. But the likeness embodied by Penny of Tina Martin would dull his calculative nature somewhat, as beautiful women are apt to do. And Penny wouldn't mention anything to diminish Martin's apparent industry knowledge.

"Good morning, Representative Martin," she offered. "We appreciate your time." Penny extended her hand to Martin as he approached. Penny intentionally prolonged her handshake, but just for an intent moment. Martin's eyes noticed the lipstick, and maybe even the eyeshadow. The chum was in the water.

"Always a pleasure, Penny," responded Martin. Penny smiled.

"Good to see you, Jim," Milton exclaimed. "It's been too long."

"Good to see you, John," replied Representative Martin.

"Lieutenant Governor West, to what do I owe this honor?" asked Martin, who couldn't keep his eyes off Penny, who had her eyes diverted, only to gaze upon West. She blinked at him and went back to engaging silently with Martin.

"Please, Jim, aren't we beyond the formalities?" West inquired and shook Martin's hand vigorously.

"I suppose so." Martin chuckled. "Y'all come in, please."

West noticed Representative Martin was unusually jovial and wondered who, or what, would have been the cause. John Milton had not been face-to-face with Martin for more than a few years, but as he discreetly scanned the office, he remembered a few details about Martin's family. As sage politicos do, they went back and forth, catching up on each other's family and interests, while Penny was absorbing a few key points for future use.

Lieutenant Governor West instinctively knew to wait until the two elder lawmakers finished their superficial ramble unimpeded. It was all part of the dance, as anyone who was versed in important business meetings would attest to. The preamble, or warmup, allowed any unnecessary tension to escape into the ether in a manageable flow.

Eventually, the dialogue gradually shifted to topics of a political nature, mostly off-colored hits on their common rivals. Then further, the seriousness of the discussion rose to an appropriate point for Martin to ask, "So tell me what I can help y'all with today?"

Without hesitation, John Milton leaned in toward Martin, accomplishing two things; first, to raise the level of seriousness, and second, to indicate to Penny and West that he had control of the conversation.

Milton smiled at Martin and quietly said, "Jim, you've done a hell of a lot for Texas over the years, everyone knows that. I won't speak for you, but I know I'm getting too long in the tooth to be running the same plays with a younger bunch, like David and Penny here." Milton paused and looked down for just an instant. "I'm not sure if you have heard, but there is a serious opportunity now for Texas to secede, and before you throw us out, let us fill you in."

Martin continued to focus on Milton and displayed no response.

"I'm listening," Martin answered.

Milton began to weave the long and complex story, lacing colorful, emotional ribbons of U.S. government malfeasance within the string of economic and social inequities, all which Martin knew, of course. The next ten minutes in Martin's office became a theater of sorts. Milton metaphorically stabbed at Martin with the outrageous costs associated with the regulatory burdens of the EPA and other agencies unfairly unleashed against the oil and gas industry. *What if*, Milton stated, again and again.

Martin's posture softened as Milton effectively painted a canvas for reclaiming the sovereignty of the Texas Republic. Penny held her breath. She was witnessing the most compelling argument in history. Her own carefully crafted words were coming out of U.S. Rep Milton's mouth at State Rep Martin and changing the course of history, not to mention her career. She felt her palms moisten, her heart race as Milton poured additional coal to the fire. The border, the fentanyl, the *lost* children, the taxes, the corruption. The case was overwhelming. And then Milton abruptly was quiet. Not a sound in the room.

"I'm sorry, Jim," Milton remarked. "It's just too close to home as they say. But more directly, Jim, we are here to help each other."

Milton adeptly shifted the conversation to his deep understanding of Martin's situation, that of a very senior lawmaker, with much influence, and the opportunity now to use his vast experience to help birth the new republic and cement his legacy. A cabinet-level position overseeing natural resources, energy and transportation, all passionately important to Martin, could be his.

Not allowing Martin to respond, Milton held up his hand and continued.

"Jim, all this may sound hard to imagine, but you need to know this. There will soon, in the coming weeks, be some news that will shake this state to its core. You will immediately know it when you see it. And when you see it, you need to call me, and we can finish this conversation. Your participation is needed. Your influence in these parts and your relationship with several representatives is something we all respect. We know this influence has taken you years to grow and cultivate, and we respect that as well. But we need you to use your influence to convince a handful of colleagues to stop thinking about their stake in all this and vote for the people, for what's right and just, and for secession when a vote is brought to the floor, and it will be. We need you to bring five or six others in your party with you. Manny has a firm tally on who stands where now, and we need you and those who believe in you to vote yes. History will list you among the brave and the patriotic. This is your chance to make your mark. Heaven knows you deserve it."

Martin remained stoic. The blood had drained from his face.

"We've taken enough of your time this morning, and I need to get to Ft. Worth right away. Can we count on you?" Milton asked as he rose and extended his hand to Martin.

"John, I am somewhat overwhelmed by the enormity of all this, but I will call you in a day or so," Martin answered. "About that other thing, something explosive…?"

"Of course, you'll need to keep this to yourself, Jim," Milton continued. "We have uncovered some shocking irregularities. I'm not at liberty to share, but I will soon."

John Martin was uncomfortable and looked to the Lt. Governor who nodded assuredly.

"If you hear anything or need information, call Miss Townsend here, she is very smart," he added, and Martin smiled sheepishly. Milton also smiled, as did Penny and David—but not at each other.

"Of course," Martin quietly replied.

Martin turned to Penny and asked, "Penny, do you have a minute?"

"Sure," Penny answered. She winked at Milton.

"LUCK IS WHAT HAPPENS WHEN PREPARATION MEETS OPPORTUNITY."

SENECA

Chapter 10

Penny approached John and David outside Representative Martin's office building with a smirk on her face.

"That didn't take long," John remarked. "Everything good?"

"Everything's good. He didn't know what hit him." She added, "Just needed to teach that man some manners." Penny had no intention of sharing anything further.

The U.S. Attorney's office in Ft. Worth, Texas, is just one of several federal agencies housed at 819 Taylor Street. The tenants of this typical twelve story government concrete cube include the IRS, Social Security, the Army Corps of Engineers, and the U.S. Attorney's. As Laci, Penny, and Charlie entered the elevator, Laci leaned into Penny and whispered, "Smells like death is among us."

The elevator doors opened to a nondescript hallway which made its way through the floor in a perfect symmetrical rectangle. Dimly lit and poorly signed, they muddled their way to the U.S. Attorney office and entered to find the offices as unsightly as the rest of the building. Charlie commented that it seemed that they were in a

Twilight Zone episode. A middle-aged, morbidly obese woman slowly raised her head to say, "Yes?"

After Laci introduced herself, Penny, and Charlie, the woman picked up her phone and entered a few keys on the keypad.

"There's someone here to see you," the woman plainly stated, and she hung up the phone. "He'll be with you in a few minutes," and she returned to her work.

"An auspicious start," Laci commented.

"Who works for whom?" Charlie asked under his breath.

From the end of the hallway a slender cut of a man in a navy suit and white button-down shirt approached, carrying a few legal notepads.

"I'm Sam, Sam Tippetts," he said smiling. He shook everyone's hand and ushered them into a small conference room down the hall.

"So, I tried to absorb everything that Congressman Milton indicated on the phone, but let's start over just so I have the information correct. Is that ok?" he asked.

"Sure," said Laci. "I'll provide the context, and we will review the documentation as we go along. How much time do you have?"

"As much as you need," Tippetts answered. "Our conversation today will be recorded, and I will need your consent for that," he continued.

All three nodded in approval and Laci provided a thorough background on herself, Penny, and Charlie, at least to the extent that Tippetts could better understand why they were in the room that day. Penny and Charlie watched and listened, sometimes exchanging glances that had little to do with the matter at hand. Penny occasionally scribbled some notes, but primarily she rifled through the stack of documents involving the crimes and activities Laci spelled out.

Penny was asked how the financial statements of Our Lady of Perpetual Light in Del Rio came into her possession. She described her history with the NGO, her activities as a board member, the children whose lives were rescued, and a list of all board members and officers. Penny recounted her relationship with Amanda Johnson and the last interaction with her in Congresswoman Mays' office before Amanda's sudden and mysterious death.

She continued receiving the locket in the mail and the attempted break in at her apartment. Tippetts asked how Penny was able to read the microchip, and Charlie told him of his associate who was technologically capable, without divulging Ryan's name. He was a bit surprised that Tippetts didn't ask for his name. But it was early. Laci regained control of the dialogue and subtly yet powerfully led the young attorney by the nose through the pile of evidence.

The hours flew by, and Tippetts glanced at his watch, then offered that a break would well serve everyone there. Laci suggested

Penny and Charlie accompany her to the car and that they take an early lunch. Tippetts assured them he would look forward to seeing them upon their return. Laci gave Penny a look and a look at the pile of information and motioned her to gather it up and take it with them.

Once in the car, Laci signaled both to remain silent, and she drove a few miles south to a local barbeque joint. Only when they were seated did she share her thoughts on the morning's proceedings.

"Well," James began, "I'm afraid we aren't being treated with an appropriate level of respect. This is not how this material is supposed to be handled, that is, if they are going to act seriously. It doesn't look good."

"What makes you say that?" inquired O'Neal.

"Throughout the conversation, I laid breadcrumbs for Tippetts, and he failed to pick up one. He's carrying the water for someone else, trust me."

Penny interjected, "Are you telling us they don't see us as serious?"

"I hate to say so, but they are not taking us very seriously," James replied. "After lunch, we'll give him every opportunity to grab this. I think it's a slam dunk, but I don't have much hope Tippetts is the right avenue. I don't want us to get arrested so maybe we just leave." The air seemed to leave the restaurant as the three sat in silence, picked at their lunch, and left.

An undistinguishable car sat in the distant corner of the restaurant facing the front door in a space anointed HANDICAP. Charlie made a mental note of the color, make, and model as Laci and Penny walked to their car in front of Charlie. The only sounds in the car returning to 819 Taylor Street that afternoon came from city traffic. Once they entered the building, Charlie handed the document case to Penny and whispered to her, "Get Laci inside and get up to the attorney's floor. I need to check on something." He winked at Penny and walked around to the side exit of the building.

Taking a long circular route back to the sedan that had followed them from the restaurant, O'Neal paused when he was close enough to make a final approach and contemplated what was about to happen. The two individuals in the car appeared to be Anglo and they looked like typical federal investigators.

The last twenty-five feet between the sedan and the nearest car caused O'Neal to consider the other possible outcomes. He shot several pictures of the car and its occupants and once he became exposed to the car in his approach, the car tore out of the parking lot, almost hitting a car as it entered the street in its rush. *Chicken shits, he thought.*

After giving the parking lot a final scan, O'Neal sent the pictures to Darst and Becker and requested plates on them for ownership. As he entered the conference room in the U.S. Attorney's office, he asked Laci and Penny to join him in the hallway to update them.

"I'll bet the plates come back as a US agency-owned vehicle," O'Neal said. "This tells me we're causing some real discomfort to somebody. And that we are on the right track. Good intuition, Laci. Good job both of you. Now, let's play it out and *get out* ASAP."

Tippetts greeted them again and the afternoon session moved along quickly. James emphasized points that were, in no uncertain terms, specific crimes. She furthered her explanation with the details surrounding Amanda's death and the bank account trails leading to Governor Harper and the White House. Her final emphasis was placed on the RICO violations. As she finished, she inquired as to his immediate supervisor and the follow-up they could expect.

A long pause followed before Tippetts responded. He turned off the recorder and carefully chose his words.

"Needless to say, these are allegations that would shake our country. The information is compelling. No, it's shocking. I will present this up the chain and we'll get back in touch with you."

"And who is your supervisor?" Laci asked again.

"My supervisor is Angela Davidson," the haughty little man squeaked out.

O'Neal choked off his anger and remarked, "Who is going to keep Penny safe while you're working up your chain?"

"Mr. O'Neal, I understand your concerns for her safety. The whistleblower statute will afford protection once the case has been opened," Tippetts responded.

"And how long will that take? Do you even realize how you sound?" remarked O'Neal, "Hell, you've just been given the case of your career, with the receipts, and you expect us to just walk out and wait for your bunch of ass-clowns to decide if it's worth pursuing? Unreal…"

"Charlie, let's allow Mr. Tippetts to lay claim to these materials and we'll be on our way," James said, and Tippetts called in an associate to tag and log the materials. Charlie watched the process silently, only occasionally glancing at Penny to check on her.

Back in the car, James said, "I'd like for us to find a quiet place to call John." Penny and Charlie agreed.

"That's too bad," responded Milton upon hearing James' recital of the day's meetings. "I was led to believe Tippetts was a real go-getter. We'll give them a week or two to get back to you, but we should talk about an alternative course of action. Today. Oh, I almost forgot, Ryan found that the car plates you asked for, belong to a regional consulting company, Maestro, who has multiple open contracts with the Department of Defense. No big surprise, eh?"

Chapter 11

O'Neal, James, and Townsend ventured into the stockyards in Ft. Worth to the Hotel Drover. Within the historic walls, there would be dining and the opportunity to design the "Plan" Milton sought. Charlie secured hotel rooms for the three, hoping that he and Penny would reconnect.

Cowhide-covered easy chairs and mesquite wood floors offered a warm, comfortable feeling to the lobby and bar at the Drover. As the trio surrounded their small table of drinks and appetizers, Charlie voiced his disgust at the U.S. Attorney's responses. Laci let Charlie vent, and only when he began to repeat himself, did she interrupt.

"Remember," Laci remarked, "the truth is like a beachball being held underwater. It will find its way to the surface. Our job is to quickly move some of the water out of the way."

The restaurant was sparsely occupied that evening, and as Charlie watchfully monitored the coming and going of patrons, the conversation jumped to mincing of the words malfeasance and misfeasance. One couldn't help noticing that Penny was experiencing a growth spurt as she drew up energy from Laci. In conversation, Penny became more declarative and convincing. She stood taller as if she wasn't tall enough already, and when she stood next to Laci, she towered over the tiny but articulate attorney. The transformation made Charlie smile on the inside. And it made him *randy*.

After Laci finished her second Cosmopolitan, she waved off a third and Penny took notice, transitioning to her water glass. Charlie had downed several iced teas, knowing he needed to remain sharp.

"Who is the investigative journalist that lives in Fredericksburg?" Penny asked. "The woman that cut her teeth in the Middle East?"

"Lana Thompson," James replied. "Brilliant idea! She has done some great work on child trafficking. I bet she jumps on this. If it's ok with you," she said looking at Charlie and Penny, "I'll get John's approval and reach out to her." Charlie and Penny smiled.

John Milton listened intently as Laci recounted the day's events in Ft. Worth and the idea of utilizing an independent journalist to push the cabal's activities into the public space. Milton asked whose idea it was, and when Laci gave credit to Penny, John chuckled. He reminded himself that he continued to underestimate this one, Penny Townsend.

As Milton hung up the phone, he mulled over the call and considered the implications of the time constraints and the imperative nature of the situation. Until now, most of the heavy lifting had been done by Charlie, Penny, and Laci. The only way he could now ensure the gang of criminals would be held to account would be through the circus known as the Congressional Oversight Committee, chaired by his friend Max Eller of Louisiana.

With pen in hand, Milton constructed an outline detailing the actors, the institutions involved, the criminal activity, and a summary of the evidence. As he laid his pen down, he wondered what the parents of Amanda Johnson, the recently murdered staffer, thought of the federal government that used their daughter as grist. He wondered if they even understood the sinister nature of her death.

The Cabernet in his glass streamed legs from the rim, and he studied the burgundy ribbon sliding down the inside of the glass for minutes. There would be no going back. The decades of work, kissing the ring, thousands of parties and fundraisers. Here and now, the next call would direct the remainder of his professional career. *Eat or be eaten.* It was in God's hands. At this stage, for him, it was a win-win.

The Congressional Oversight Committee has oversight of the executive branch, including the numerous U.S. federal agencies. Congressional oversight includes reviewing, monitoring, and supervising federal agencies, programs, activities, and policy implementation. Congress exercises this power largely through its congressional committee system. Oversight also occurs in congressional activities and contexts, which is investigated by select committees, and reviews and studies agencies and staff.

As usual, Eller was happy to hear from Milton, and after the two caught up with topics these two enjoyed and shared on a personal level, like, duck hunting, Milton adeptly transitioned the conversation. In detail, Milton reconstructed the web of conspirators and at every place of a criminal act, hung the critical evidential data to provide receipts. Milton introduced Charlie O'Neal, Penny Townsend, Laci James, and Michael Darst to Eller in a manner that entirely legitimized the sources. He seamlessly processed the chain of events and ended the explanation by saying, "Max, this cannot stand..."

Many seconds of silence were followed by Eller's response, "John, how long have we known each other?"

"Since the *first* Bush fiasco, the Gulf War," John answered.

"Yeah, that's about right," Eller said. "I don't have any doubt about everything you've told me. And I am sure you're completely disappointed with the U.S. Attorney." Eller paused. "I'm grateful you called me on this, before calling the Speaker." Again, a lengthy pause followed. "If you can assure me that the material will be in my office tomorrow, I'll schedule a committee meeting. I'll brief the Speaker tomorrow, but it will take at least three weeks for the committee to meet. Tell me if that will work for you," Eller continued.

"Max," John answered, "we must assume the U.S. Attorney's office will leak it, and we may need to use an outside resource to ensure this information reaches the public. We have discussed using an independent journalist to create a sense of urgency. Hope you understand if it leaks from that hose?"

"That would be unfortunate," Eller replied, "but understandable. Can you overnight the materials?"

"Of course, Max," John replied. "Hope we'll stay in close communication on this?"

"Believe it, John," Max stated. "These sons-a-bitches… it's time to clean this up. And John, one more thing. Those unelected weasels at the U.S. Attorney's office? If they don't pursue this within two weeks, we'll subpoena their communications and throw their asses in a sling. Give my regards to your bride, John."

Conversation at the table in the Hotel Drover descended to easy topics, such as government employees and appetizers. Beautiful salads glided onto their table, followed by plump cuts of beef tenderloin and creamed spinach. Penny and Charlie exchanged several glances, and Penny's foot, freed from her Navy leather pump, found its way to the back of Charlie's calf, where it gently stroked his leg for several minutes. Dinner was luxuriously long and before dessert, Charlie asked to be excused for the evening.

He covered the tab and headed for his room ahead of Penny and Laci, thinking Penny might call when she had reached her room.

Laci was not clueless about what was unfolding between Charlie and Penny. She thought it sweet. She and Penny continued their conversation for almost an hour when she asked Penny if she could call it a night.

The blackout curtains were drawn, and the thermostat was lowered to sixty-five degrees. O'Neal was on the bed with his slacks on watching a news channel when his phone buzzed.

"Did I wake you?" Penny whispered.

Charlie chuckled. "Not quite."

"Can you come up?" Penny gingerly asked. "I think I leak," she implored. "Do you have tools? Can you check out my plumbing?"

That caught Charlie by surprise and sent him into roaring laughter. "Yes, ma'am, I'm glad you asked," Charlie replied. "I'd be happy to."

As Charlie reached Penny's floor, he paused at the entrance to the stairwell to check the hallway, and his pulse. He chuckled to himself, finding his heart rate elevated, and with good reason, he thought. He knocked once on the door, with meaning. Penny unlocked the door and cracked it open only slightly.

"Who is it?" she meekly asked.

"Come on now," Charlie replied.

The door swung open and through the light cast by the window, Charlie vaguely traced Penny's silhouette through her thin nighty. He reached around her waist to bring her close. The room was faintly lit, and chilly. Penny knew that Charlie liked a cold room, and the anticipation almost caused her to quiver.

The two became one and eventually dozed off in each other's arms. Charlie was awakened by Penny delicately stroking him. Petting.

"Tell me about Sophia, Charlie?" Penny whispered.

Charlie turned to lie on his back and gather his thoughts.

"I'm not sure which part you want to hear, but Sophia was mystical," Charlie began. "Sophia was a curandera, and if you know what that means, it's probably the best way to know who she was. She knew things, things that everyone else, including me, didn't know or see. Why are you asking?"

Penny took a breath. "The more I know about you, Charlie, the more I need to know," Penny answered.

"Me thinks you know plenty already," Charlie quipped.

Time became non-existent for Penny and Charlie until his alarm buzzed at 6 the next morning.

To better understand the liberal mindset, one can directly refer to *radical* Richard Cloward and *radical* Frances Piven, both professors at the Columbia University School of Social Work. The strategy known as Cloward-Piven was outlined in a May 1966 article in the liberal magazine *The Nation* titled: "The Weight of the Poor: A Strategy to End Poverty." One might just call it a *license to steal.*

Cloward and Piven's article focused on *subversively* compelling the Democratic Party, which in 1966 controlled the presidency and both houses of the United States Congress, to "redistribute income" to help the poor, and themselves. They righteously stated that full enrollment of those eligible for welfare, "would produce bureaucratic disruption in welfare agencies and fiscal disruption in local and state governments to *deepen existing divisions among elements in the big-city Democratic coalition, namely the remaining white middle class, the working-class ethnic groups and the growing minority poor."*

To avoid a further weakening of that historic coalition, a national Democratic administration would be constrained to advance a federal solution to poverty "*that would override local welfare failures. Yet, they (Who exactly is they?) continue to fund local class and racial conflicts, and local revenue dilemmas only worsened."* It wasn't a solution to poverty; it was only another heavy brick thrown through the glass window in the wall of shame.

The *supposed* objective of this strategy was to wipe out poverty by establishing a guaranteed annual income, which is inflationary. Because the ideal of individual social and economic mobility had deep roots, even activists seemed reluctant to call for national programs to eliminate poverty by the distribution of others' income and assets.

It was written that Cloward and Piven started it. Some crazy outer-limits joke. They proposed to create a crisis in the current welfare system by exploiting the gap between welfare law and practice, which would ultimately bring about its collapse, and replace it with a system of guaranteed annual income. They hoped to accomplish this by informing the poor of their "*rights* to welfare assistance, *encouraging* them to apply for *benefits,* and, in effect, *overloading* an already *overburdened bureaucracy*."

Penny objected, saying, "No one said *WHOA*! No one said *STOP*! It wasn't politically correct, although it was fiscally, ethically, and morally correct. No one said *WHOA*! Please, somebody say it! WHOA…"

A country with NO ASSETS cannot defend itself. We're there. And tax-payer money continues to drizzle into the Ukraine, for example, and into the pockets of vast and various government employees. Patriotic Americans, citizens, are being squeezed to their death.

Remember Mao Zedong?

Or, Joseph Stalin. "…cruel efforts under Stalin to impose [*his* will] collectivism (Communism) and tamp down Ukrainian nationalism left an estimated 3.9 million dead." Vladimir Lenin—mass murder during his Red Terror killed 1.4 MILLION.

Students of the strategy, which include a recent secretary of state and U.S. president, have sought the benefits systems to gain control and increase their power. The result of the strategy is that current and previous administrations have been filled with tens of thousands of unelected staff determined to inflict their ideology on a population they perceive as unintelligible, uninformed, and breakable.

President Michael Robinson was an avid and outspoken advocate of the Cloward-Piven strategy, not to bring a guaranteed income to the masses, but to move the United States to the precursor of communism, socialism, and autocracy. Robinson made his first indelible mark by handicapping private healthcare insurance and requiring citizens to carry insurance, effectively driving the less fortunate population to government platforms. A snake oil salesman, Robinson promised, "You can keep your doctor, keep your insurance, and your costs will go down." All three promises, of course, vanished with the next rising of the sun. A critic in the chamber called him out to his face. *Liar!*

Strategically, Robinson and his team of power-hungry bureaucrats had effectively gained control of twenty percent of the U.S. economy, diverting revenue streams from intended recipients to the criminal cabal of traitors the White House wanted to grease.

Hollywood/Hollyweird came to town, D.C., *in the middle of the night.* It was a carnival with trimmings, clowns, jesters, lions, and con artists.

America was experiencing how the water in the pot was slowly being brought to a boil from the frog's point of view. Rumblings were heard in several states to convene a Convention of States, as the Constitution provides in Article 5.

Article 5 states; *The Congress, whenever two-thirds of both houses shall deem it necessary, shall propose amendments to this Constitution, or, on the application of the legislatures of two-thirds of the several states, shall call a convention for proposing amendments, which, in either case, shall be valid, as part of this Constitution, when ratified by the legislatures of three-fourths of the several states, or by conventions in three fourths thereof, as the one or the other mode of ratification may be proposed by the Congress; provided that no amendment which may be made before the year one thousand eight hundred and eight shall in any manner affect the first and fourth clauses in the ninth section of the first article; and that no state, without its consent, shall be deprived of its equal suffrage in the Senate.*

Article 5 proved the genius of the writers of the U.S. Constitution. If the government became too unruly and inflicted too much pain on the citizenry, the states had the power to affect their collective will by having a direct path to amend the Constitution.

The requirements are justifiably steep for a convention to be brought. The results of a convention of states have far-reaching, fundamental implications.

Uncertainty whirled about the United States, creating an ominous, virtue-less cycle, which generated pent-up nervousness. Financial markets saw volatility swings that bloodied the average investor. Speculation swept into precious metals markets and college campuses predictably swarmed with professional protesters. Most Americans never altered their daily routines, burdened by their inability to leave the workplace, financially overburdened by soaring, *silent* inflation. *Media* were slow to honestly portray the fragile nature of the country, adeptly constructing the diversions to keep the children at the magic show *properly* distracted by sock puppets. Men dressed as women, wanting to be called "they."

The darkened turns unfolding across the country were closely followed by Milton, Darst, and Lt. Governor West. Governor Harper had just recently stopped his usual communications with West. The smoke of a distant bonfire was in the air.

The general who wins the battle makes many calculations in his temple before the battle is fought. The general who loses makes but few calculations beforehand.

– Sun Tzu

Chapter 12

The Republic of Texas declared independence from the Republic of Mexico on March 2, 1836. It applied for annexation to the United States the same year but was rejected by the United States Secretary of State. At that time, a majority of the Texan population favored the annexation of the Republic by the United States. The leadership of both major U.S. political parties (Democrats and Whigs) opposed the introduction of Texas—a vast slave-holding region—into the volatile political climate of the pro-slavery and anti-slavery sectional controversies in Congress. Moreover, they wished to avoid a war with Mexico, whose maniacal and rebellious government had outlawed slavery and refused to acknowledge the sovereignty of its uncontrollable northern province.

With Texas's economic fortunes declining by the early 1840s, the president of the Texas Republic, the legendary Sam Houston, arranged sweet talks with Mexico to explore the possibility of securing official recognition of independence.

In the 1840s, global oversupply caused a crash in the price of cotton, one of the country's dependable and rewarding export commodities. The situation led to labor shortages, reduced tax revenue, large national debts, and a diminished Texas militia. In his first address to Congress in a special session on June 1, 1841, President Tyler proposed the possibility of a sort of merger, Texas annexation, by announcing his intention to cobble a committee to craft a feasibility study to pursue an expansionist agenda to preserve the balance between state and national authority and to protect American institutions, including slavery, to avoid sectional conflict as if anyone understood any of that *word salad.* Tyler's closest advisors counseled him that obtaining Texas would be the jewel of his presidency and assure him a second term in the White House. It became a deeply personal obsession for the president, who viewed the acquisition of Texas as the "primary objective of his administration" and quite a poppy in his lapel.

With the Webster–Ashburton Treaty ratified in 1843, the administration authorized Representative Thomas W. Gilmer of Virginia to make the case for annexation to the American electorate. In a widely circulated open letter, Gilmer announced the executive branch's designs for Texas and described Texas as a panacea for North-South conflict, and an economic boon to all commercial interests.

The slavery issue, however divisive, would be left for the states to decide as per the U.S. Constitution. One could just drop in *abortion* where slavery is mentioned and have the same circular, really *ovoidal*, insanity that rewriting history engenders with time to percolate, and a press on nitrous oxide—laughing gas. Domestic tranquility and national security would result from an annexed Texas; the Texas Republic left outside American jurisdiction would imperil the Union. Tyler adroitly arranged the resignation of his anti-annexation Secretary of State Daniel Webster, and on June 23, 1843, appointed Abel P. Upshur, a Virginia states' rights champion and ardent proponent of Texas annexation.

This cabinet seat shift signaled Tyler's intent to pursue Texas annexation aggressively. US Secretary of State Upshur vigorously exhorted Texas diplomats to begin annexation talks, finally dispatching an appeal to President Sam Houston in January 1844. In the appeal, Upshur assured Houston that the political climate in the United States was currently amenable to Texas statehood and that a two-thirds majority in the Senate could be obtained to ratify a Texas treaty.

Texans were hesitant to pursue a US-Texas treaty without a written commitment to military defense from Mother America since a full-scale military attack by Mexico seemed likely when the negotiations became public. If ratification of the annexation measure stalled in the U.S. Senate, Texas could face a bloody war alone against Mexico.

Although he lacked constitutional authority, Secretary Upshur provided the use of military defense, and President Houston, responding to urgent calls for annexation from the Texas Congress of December 1843, authorized the reopening of annexation negotiations. Exerting power well beyond Constitutional authority had been practiced by non-elected bureaucrats for a long time, across many administrations.

"Knock knock,"

"Who's there?"

"Very funny. Ok, Nobel," Penny said.

"Nobel who?"

"Nobel… that's why I knocked."

"Good one. I'll be down in five."

In the most recent state legislative session, Texas State Representative Jensen Eichholz attempted, through proper parliamentarian procedures, a ballot initiative through the Republican party to be a part of the most recent March primary to ask voters if Texas should regain its independence through a non-binding referendum. To become part of the ballot, the referendum would require 100,000 signatures. A simply stated referendum, *Should Texas be allowed to reassert its ability to become an independent nation,* the voter could express his choice, as constitutionally provided, to select the government desired.

The petition signatures obtained vastly exceeded the requirement of the party to be placed on the primary ballot, but the Republican party flatly rejected the petition, and the Texas Supreme Court, without any rationale, sided with the establishment party leaving the independence-seeking masses without recourse within the legal framework. *Nothing to see here, folks*, as the traffic cop would say. *You never see the bus that hits you.* That's what Sophia would say.

Texas journalist Lana Thompson, renowned for her courageous and clean reporting (... all the news that's fit to print, gathered from places no one dares to explore), had in exquisite journalist fashion agreed to meet with O'Neal and Townsend at an off-the-grid wine bar east of Fredericksburg to hear the story. She had been warned by O'Neal that they would be followed. Odds are Lana would be as well. Penny and Charlie were anxiously awaiting her at a small table in a dimly lit corner when Lana came around the corner and slid in. Penny and Lana exchanged gracious professional compliments, having followed one another on social media.

Charlie chopped that all up and went to work. "Before we get too far, I want to let you know, Lana, that we have a guy named Demi, who will be calling you." O'Neal calmly leaned in on one side of her, while Penny leaned in on the reporter's other side. They filled her in on the mission, masked by the live band's music.

"You have placed yourself in a potentially dangerous spot." This, of course, caused Lana to laugh almost over the band. They all three laughed. "The information on this thumb drive implicates people at the highest level who are at risk of complete exposure now and they know it. They have nothing to lose so they're morally bankrupt and dangerous. Everything you say on any social media platform will be closely AI-monitored so please be discreet. Demi is outside already to ensure your safety. If you sense something, a hunch, anything, dial the last call received on this flip phone and Demi will appear. Try not to be startled." He smiled. For only a few seconds he wondered what Sophia would think about all this. And Susan, bless her heart. He turned back to Lana. "If you haven't lately, you may want to read up on the Nazi infiltrator Henry Kissinger, and if you think you see the picture, read it again."

"Hey," she began… O'Neal put up his hand to silence her.

"Remember in the Book of Esther?" he asked her. She did not and with eyes wide she turned to Penny.

"Who knows but that you have come to your royal position for such a time as this?" Penny spoke quietly reaching to take her hand, opened it, palm up. O'Neal slid the burner phone and a thumb drive across the small table to the journalist.

He nodded, said thank you, and commented, "Things will never be the same for you if you choose to do this." Lana and Penny nodded in unison. Lana looked down at the thumb drive, the center of the bloody universe cradled in the palm of her hand.

"Mr. O'Neal, you don't strike me to be a man of much nonsense," Lana said. "Why me?"

Charlie grinned. "I didn't choose you," he answered. "She did." He pointed to Penny.

"Lana," began Penny, "we got the goods. We got it all, no photo-shopped bullshit. We know child trafficking is especially important to you, and when you put your eyes on these materials, you'll know. Just report it. Do your job and report the news. *Ta-Da!*"

"Really?" Lana's eyes flooded with tears. She was physically and emotionally exhausted, but still beautiful. She just needed some rest.

"It will blow your mind. My number is also on the flip phone in case you have any questions. Please call me if I can help you in any way."

Lana intensely studied Penny. Lana looked at both of them. She wiped a tear. "I will do my best to not disappoint you."

"Yep," O'Neal said. "We were sorta counting on that."

"Yep," Penny agreed.

Lana gave a *thumbs up*, and she was gone.

Darst and Congressman Milton had readied the multi-pronged strategy to eventually re-install the Texas Constitution in Austin as the governing framework for Texas, a sovereign nation, to implement trade agreements with the U.S. federal government, Canada, and Mexico and provide low-cost contracts to the U.S. government to lease all facilities on Texas dirt on an interim basis.

Darst scheduled the final meeting of leadership, off-grid, at his ranch near Gonzales. Darst and his late wife breathed new air into a brilliant work of art on the Guadalupe River that housed their family history, their children, friends, and community. Holidays in that historic house were magical.

Darst met Sue at college. He was determined to graduate, and she was an uptown girl, hunting, if you catch my drift.

He was in love with a girl named Sue. He couldn't get her out of his mind. He had some shite job on a rig out in west Texas, and he grew up fast. He talked her into marrying him one night. After drinking, in the back seat of her car, she rocketed to the moon for the first time, and she said, "Yes, I'll marry you." Who knew?

"First, I have to finish school," he told her.

"He didn't have enough money for the semester so he applied for a grant and a school loan and when he gets the money," she explained to her family, "he'll pay for the semester and then we can talk about getting married."

Darst was studying to be a chemist for the minerals industry. He'd just started with a company, and it was pretty decent money. He had considered skipping school and working in the oil patch for a while. Sue would have no part of it.

"It's twenty thousand dollars. I could do both if I focused on those two with my head down. Every minute of my day would be consumed. I could do it." Sue would have no part of that either.

So, they broke up. And they were both miserable. Darst refused to call her, and Sue refused to answer his calls. Darst finished college, paid back his school debt, and chose some graduate classes that interested him, non-matriculating sans the diploma, and that combination gave him exactly what he needed to go the next step. He took Business Law, Economics and Ballroom Dancing.

The night before, Darst had his first lucid dream. And the following morning, he walked into Merrill Lynch and purchased a million shares of INTEL, the budding semiconductor hub trading on the pink sheets at $.02 a share and he plopped down $20,000. He bought a ring and then hunted down the love of his life. Every year she either traded it, usually for a larger diamond or different shape, or changed settings and reset them, never quite satisfied. Not hard to please, a sociable CEO wife, but Sue could disembowel you if you stepped on her toes, literally and figuratively. Darst was at the height of his career having had the wit, foresight, and earnings, not to mention that dream prodding him to position INTEL, to buy the largest chunk of the oil company he had toiled at, and now owned. And Sue told him when to sell it.

"The microchip was what brought me to this place. And the microchip will fulfill what God deemed my journey and mission. I'm exactly where I'm supposed to be. Mission accomplished."

Have I outlived my usefulness now? Michael Darst wondered whenever he got a little insecure. Sue gone, the kids gone, the dog almost gone, bless her heart, and I pray that the mission is successful, that the people will participate in the transition in a logical and meaningful way without riots and bloodshed. One never knows what the Left will get up to. I will be sure that two items will be reversed immediately, and I will always call out Robinson, that weasel, to his face. I will re-criminalize propaganda, and I will re-criminalize insider trading. And I will personally sue that bastard that got paid millions to seal that fraud's records and papers. Robinson and that attorney are both guilty of noose-worthy treason, all kinds of RICO violations, and Amanda Johnson's murder and cover-up. Amen.

INTEL paid out $3,000,000. Sue wasted most of it. The kids were eager for their fair share, and this guy wasn't eager to turn over $.05 of it. There was a clause in her will and schedule of dispersion of tangible assets stating his power to redirect cash dispersion to the issues of said unions, also referred to as grandchildren, and great grandchildren. A family dynasty, if you will. The kids were going to blow a gasket. They should have been nicer to him. He laughed. It was funny and sad, a perfect confluence.

It struck O'Neal how vastly different the tone at this stage of the process was, compared to the prior policy meetings. The discussions now centered on implementation rather than the previous perspective of strategies. Only a few hours were necessary for the entire team to be briefed in preparation for the upcoming release of the overwhelming evidence certain to shake the country, if not the entire world.

Sophia taught him that pedophilia is like Sociopathy. A symptom. Incurable. The first cut is the deepest. The first snort, or first high, is the highest. That's it. Is that all there is? Yes. That's it. And now you're addicted to another mouth to feed. You'll chase it. The memory of that first time is the engine driving this yearning. The mice and the pellets. Only one mouse died. The one whose brain was wired like the pedophile's. The rat. Looking for the next pellet. "Jonesing."

The effects of the upcoming contentious presidential election rippled through Texas like water across a pond only faster. Darst was certain that the governor had no choice but to resist the movement to see Texas regain its independence, and although he would be fighting off impeachment and soon criminal charges, he proved his resilience with the public again and again. Governor Harper had again demonstrated political mastery in his ambiguity and deflection.

Nationally, voting irregularities with voting machines and ballot box stuffing in swing states were expected to resurface, due in part to the abysmal performance of President Robinson and his family's grifting. The indecency of the administration's façade angered half of the country and was conveniently ignored by the biased, compliant media which essentially partnered with the administration and strove to portray the president as the only hope for the crumbling republic. It was all theater. Masks and make-up and costumes and scenes, so many scenes. Academy Awards awarded to themselves. They legalized propaganda. No one said a word.

The Republican presidential nominee, an educated woman who served in the Marine Corps in Iraq and subsequently as a U.S. Senator for two terms, called for an investigation of the White House and massive reform within the government. Threatened with elimination by the fiery brunette with feasible conservative values and policies, that she called modest and civilized, were entire federal agencies and cabinet departments, causing significant concern for the establishment. An All-Alarm Situation.

This was Andriana Walker Bain, the highly favored Republican presidential nominee. Bain was raised in Clinton, Massachusetts, the eldest child of a firefighter and middle school teacher. Andriana attended The College of the Holy Cross in Worcester on a Naval ROTC scholarship. Under the Marine option, she attended the

Mountain War Training Center in California after her sophomore year and Officer Candidate School prior to her senior year.

As Andriana graduated, the United States was deeply involved in the war in Iraq, and as a newly commissioned 2nd Lieutenant, was immediately deployed to Iraq where she commanded a platoon of sixteen Marines. Due to her relative inexperience in command, Bain was mentored by a more experienced senior non-commissioned officer, an anthropology doctoral candidate, who served with her in the Middle East. Later, Bain shared with open-sourced media that the strength of the USMC non-commissioned officer culture and tradition was, she believed, a unique advantage over most all other militaries. A history major, Bain became enthralled with the rise and fall of earlier republics through others who sought the same knowledge. Her deeply held belief was that the United States was entering a perilous and lethal decline as did all republics of the past. This perspective drove Bain to nobly devote her career to the constitutional republic to which she swore an oath. She found that many independent thinkers and scholars were all arriving at the same conclusion. And that is, we are the old civilization, we are so over and must be expunged to make room for the new civilization, washing ashore now, uninvited, like smelts.

The rallies held by the candidate Bain attracted many times more attendees than ever seen by presidential candidates. The crowds were emotional and were described by the press as traitorous and potentially violent. Reporting by the media distorted the enthusiasm demonstrated by the huge crowds of peaceful, patriotic Americans coming out to be a part of the reform movement in cities across the country.

The enthusiasm was unprecedented and undeniable, but the media recognized the threat and used their platforms to twist and obfuscate the reality that Americans were awakening to the opportunity to take their country back from the handful of war-mongering globalists that pulled the levers of control and who are about to be exposed. But was it too late? Had the blind termites irreparably damaged the infrastructure by chewing it and reducing it to sawdust, never to stand tall and indivisible, never to be reimagined or extolled. And the lies, formidable, salacious, malicious, lies told with impunity. Calumny. Sharia. Deadly.

Over the summer months approaching the election, the crowds continued to swell, and the approval ratings of the Republican candidate soared. It appeared that the second term of President Robinson was very much in play. Andriana Bain was a classic beauty, raw talent with that classic education, with time spent at Oxford, and perfect bones, she was known for her smooth and confident gait, of all things. Andriana, almost everyone called her Andee, was a common-sense populist, with a simple *If it ain't broke, don't fix it* economic leaning. Doesn't like debt and doesn't want debt. Or, war. "No more war" pink hats waved enthusiastically, along with *ABORTION: figure it out*, and the much acclaimed "Avoid Conception" campaign, that fell on deaf ears. The woman who wanted to be Queen. She grew in boldness as she recalled personally touring every mental health facility in Maricopa County when no one knew her, no one seemed to mind the conditions for reform as the crowds became more raucous and energetic.

The word Nationalist is now a curse word while the F-word is the most over-used word in the English language. Or all languages combined. Hope for renewed liberty was palpable.

As the Republican reformer walked onto the stage at a rally in Chicago, in early September, at a large capacity venue, Wrigley Field, crowds stood in line for a better part of the day and roared its approval. "You can't always get what you want," the Rolling Stones's iconic classic rock song, blared through the packed ballpark as the candidate clapped and pointed at nearby attendees.

The passionate supporters were mostly unaware that the candidate posed a direct threat to the leviathan military-industrial complex, and that forces were being unleashed to discredit the candidate and destabilize her campaign. Her prior military experience would soon help her avoid certain unforeseen tragedies.

Rumors began to swirl of an inside job to create chaos in the Republican party and allow Robinson to waltz to his second inauguration. Establishment Republicans and liberal DC pundits fueled the fictional but destructive gossip and worse, the malicious and condemning lies concocted to maim or kill an opponent. Calumny again. When yes means no and east is west, and everyone is lying, robbing, hurting, killing, aborting, and defacing everything that is good and solid and holy… then, what?

The final two months before the November election were filled with media-promoted lies regarding infighting and unresolved core issues within the Republican party. Right-wing groups threatened a revolt, and the Black Lives Matter group grabbed the opportunity to appear as a stabilizing force for the teetering republic. Financial markets and many banks threatened their closing, which only exacerbated fear in major cities. All but the most fervent voters were in a quandary of uncertainty, to the delight of the Robinson campaign and the mainstream media.

In Democrat-controlled cities, looting and rioting broke out, in the fashion of those following the George Floyd death, all promoted and funded by a globalist who had long sought the destruction of the capitalist society. Professionals amassed and arrived on time on buses to a particular city that would in just two days experience the worse mass violence and destruction. It looked like a movie set.

Pallets of incendiaries magically appeared near structures, delivered as ordered, like pizza at midnight, that were soon engulfed in flames. The already neutered police departments proved entirely incapable of controlling the incoming buses of paid protesters spewing hate, lighting firecrackers, setting everything they could on fire. Chaos (Cloward & Piven). The orchestration was masterful and by the time inept Democratic leadership brought real law enforcement to bear, the buses were long gone, heading for the next city. Paid protesters, *legal* propaganda, what could go wrong?

As the date of the general election approached, Bain feverishly traveled from one swing state to another. The state Republican team in Michigan, competing for Michigan's fifteen electoral votes, provided ample polling data to Bain's team to justify a half day in Dearborn for a rally just before election day. Dearborn allowed Bain to step directly into the historic birthplace of Henry Ford and the tens of thousands of now disenfranchised union workers while logistically only a thirty-minute drive from Detroit's airport.

While the Interstate Highway 94 provides three lanes in the southwest direction from Detroit to Dearborn, in late morning traffic, Bain's caravan of SUVs snaked effortlessly amidst light traffic at speeds well over the posted speed limit, as was the usual practice. As the group pulled aside a non-descript pickup truck, an undetected drone lifted from the pickup bed and dropped alongside the caravan eighteen inches above the pavement.

The pickup allowed Bain's vehicle and its escorts to gradually pull away but in an instant, the explosive-laden drone slipped under Bain's SUV and detonated, sending the vehicle skyward. Flipping in midair, the armored Tahoe landed on its roof and slid along the elevated portion of I95 until it finally rested upon a sand-filled construction barrier. When the smoke and dust cleared, every occupant of the SUV was either injured or killed. Andriana Bain was life-flighted to DMC Detroit Receiving Hospital, a Level 1 Trauma Center.

Johnny Cash's iconic song says "Bad news travels like wildfire, good news travels slow…" With only a week to election day, the national media pontificated at length the unprecedented situation of a presidential candidate whose health and viability were totally in question. *What if Bain dies after election day or is unable to serve? What about her running mate? How could the Secret Service allow this to happen? Aren't our political leaders safe?* Little concern was raised about her actual well-being, or that of her husband and two children, or the tragic loss of the driver, a seasoned and respected Secret Service Agent who left a family of five behind. Just another day making the donuts.

Amid the widespread chaos across the country, Lana Thompson concluded her due diligence on the vast material provided by Penny and Charlie. Charlie was right. From nowhere, unmarked SUVs were following Lana and coincidentally, her home security alarm system was triggered more than once. Demi closely watched Lana and twice directly confronted the unwanted thugs. Lana finally contacted the Gillespie County Sheriff, who knew Lana and her unique risk profile and agreed to post a deputy outside her home.

Penny received several calls from Lana for explanations, and Penny knew from the conversations that Lana was nervously putting the finishing touches on an irrefutable article destined to reach around the globe. Demi remained ever vigilant and, in the shadows, ready to bring swift and silent protection to the journalist who would expose the far-reaching scandal to the world.

Lana suggested to Penny that the information should be shared on a national cable news network. The suggestion was relayed to John Milton who enthusiastically agreed. The U.S. Attorney's office in Ft. Worth remained silent. Milton, Darst, and James grew increasingly nervous that leaks had occurred, and maneuvering had begun to cover the tracks left by Robinson, Mays, and Harper.

The new levels of chaos brought all Americans to their phones and televisions more than ever. Small riots broke out in cities and towns previously only known for a contribution to the country in a past generation. Gangs coming over the border illegally and in packs like wolves were pillaging the villages and raping the land as well as citizens. No one was saying anything.

It seemed that tensions couldn't get higher, that the United States was approaching the proverbial tipping point. The future implications for Robinson's, May's, and Harper's families, of course, were enormous.

In Texas, state politicians scurried to usurp power and line their pockets with promises and IOUs in times of chaos as this, here, now.

Lobbyists were suddenly seeing new alignment with many state legislators, and "find axiom related to confidence growing as the crowd swells."

Under the provisions of the Texas Constitution, the lieutenant governor is president of the Texas Senate. Unlike some states senates and the U.S. senate, the lieutenant governor regularly presides over the chamber rather than delegating this function to the president pro tempore or a majority leader. By the rules of the senate, the lieutenant governor establishes all special and standing committees, appoints all chairpersons and members, and assigns all senate legislation to the committee of his choice. The lieutenant governor decides all questions of parliamentary procedure in the senate and has broad discretion with senate procedural rules.

The lieutenant governor has a vast umbrella over several statutory bodies, such as the Legislative Budget Board, Legislative Council, Legislative Audit Committee, Legislative Board, and the Legislative Council, with considerable sway over state programs, the budget, and policy. The lieutenant governor also has the pleasure of watching over the Legislative Redistricting Board (together with the speaker of the house, attorney general, comptroller, and land commissioner), which is charged with adopting a redistricting plan for the Texas House of Representatives, Texas Senate, or U.S. House of Representatives.

The day before Lana Thompson's explosive report was released, John Milton and Michael Darst flew to Austin to meet with Texas Lieutenant Governor West, Attorney General Lindemann, along with Manny Elizondo, their lobbyist. The Texas lieutenant governor knew full well that his time had come, and all the painful years of standing behind Governor Harper would soon be over.

The unthinkable had happened—the tiny band had secured irrefutable and verified sources to connect President Robinson, Texas Congresswoman Mays, and Texas Governor Lambert to offshore bank accounts in Panama and a network of NGOs all acting in a coordinated manner to receive and relocate thousands of illegal immigrant children, some infants. Most of all, only because she was a lone ranger and Penny's dear friend, who Penny owed so much, they would find out who killed Amanda and who ordered it.

After their final meeting with Lana, Charlie and Penny drove eastward on Highway 290 toward Johnson City, the home of Lyndon B. Johnson, the 36th President, who said upon the signing of the civil rights act of 1964, "We'll have those niggers voting Democratic for 200 years." As expected, Charlie and Penny were followed by an unmarked SUV as Charlie's truck turned eastward. O'Neal knew that Road 205 south of 290 had several low water crossings, and he knew that recent rainfall might cause some of the hill country creeks to swell. He also knew that his truck had a higher clearance than the following SUV. *Risky*, he thought, but he leaned forward and picked up speed as he approached the turn onto 205 toward a little-known low-water crossing.

"Penny, you may want to have that cigarette now," he muttered, eyes fixed on the rear-view mirror.

"Why is that?" Penny asked.

"Trust me," O'Neal remarked in his uber-serious voice.

"Well, if you insist," Penny remarked, as she searched her gear for a freshly rolled cigarette and fished out a lighter.

The road was rocky and bumpy, lots of mud splashing. Her toes were perched on the edge of the dashboard, like two hands with talons for stability, toes painted to match her fingernails, of course. She lit her joint, slowly inhaled, and methodically exhaled the magic smoke in O'Neal's direction. He smiled but never moved his eyes from the twisting blacktop ahead and the mirror reflection of anything pursuing from the rear.

As they descended to the water crossing, the nearby warning post indicated the water was ten to twelve inches deep, but more importantly, it was moving rapidly. O'Neal glanced downstream to envision where they might land if swept away and he pressed the accelerator. The initial impact when they entered the crossing shot water in every direction, the pickup's momentum pushing it well into the crossing, and O'Neal instinctively stomped his foot on the gas. The rear of the pickup swerved violently, but eventually, they crawled out of the crossing.

Several hundred yards behind Charlie and Penny, the SUV, driven by a goon unfamiliar with the terrain, was cautiously rounding every sharp turn and when they slowly approached the water crossing, they saw the wet tracks on the far side created by O'Neal's pickup.

The driver activated the four-wheel drive and slowly entered the crossing. The attempt seemed successful until the SUV was mid-crossing when the current began pushing the vehicle sideways and pulled it downstream. As the tires lost traction, the occupants quickly understood that they were at the mercy of the swollen stream. The vehicle traveled nearly one hundred feet before a young cypress tree stopped the SUV's downward travel.

Taking no chances, Charlie and Penny crisscrossed their way back to Victoria. Retrieving her phone from her Faraday bag, Penny had multiple voice messages from her boss that grew more intense and even frantic. O'Neal called Darst with a progress report that caused Darst to erupt into laughter. Darst advised O'Neal that it would be prudent to detour slightly south and meet with a friend's employees near Kenedy to exchange vehicles. O'Neal acknowledged his instructions and slapped the phone shut. Penny and Charlie chuckled, and Penny dropped her phone back into the bag, providing them movement that couldn't be tracked.

Upon reaching the small town of Kenedy in south Texas, O'Neal stopped at La Bahia Energy field office which was owned by a close friend of Darst. They were guided into a large shop where O'Neal parked his pickup and overhead doors glided down to hide the vehicle from prying eyes. O'Neal and Townsend were escorted into a conference room within the regional office building. News channels were watched intently, and nothing was mentioned to give the pair any indication their material had been reported. Charlie was handed a set of vehicle keys and they walked out into the vast shop area.

The couple was directed to a rough but operable La Bahia vehicle and they transferred their gear and resumed their journey. Charlie texted the journalist to request an update and was instantly rewarded with a response. *Watch cable news tomorrow!!* O'Neal managed to drive for an hour or more before he found a motel in Cuero that suited him.

Penny was awakened by the sound of Charlie entering the hotel room, and the smell of fresh coffee succeeded in rousing her from a long night of little rest. She grabbed the remote and turned the television on to see major news announcements from a major national cable television channel announcing the report from Lana Thompson exposing the largest scandal to ever shake the United States.

The sitting U.S. president, a U.S. congresswoman, and the governor of Texas were embroiled in siphoning funds through a reputable Catholic charity, trafficking immigrant children and fentanyl, and colluding with a Mexican drug cartel. Dozens of Washington, D.C. officials were also listed as active participants in the child trafficking enterprise. The news channel personnel were shocked and were struggling to follow their teleprompters. Both Charlie's and Penny's phones were ringing nonstop.

"How's your day going so far, Ms. Townsend, and how's that cup of java?" Charlie inquired with a wink.

"Perfect." Penny closed her eyes, exhaled, and whispered, "It's all perfect. Damn, you're really good."

"Ready to go?"

"Ten minutes."

The basketball court at Westlake High School in Austin was covered with middle schoolers preparing for the final cheer competition of the morning. Laci and Scott James were glued to their daughter as she completed her stretching and warmup when Laci's phone alerted her. She looked down at her phone to read the news headlines of the national scandal and she held her phone out to her husband Scott to read. He glanced through the article and grinned at Laci, who pocketed her phone and yelled out to her daughter in her support.

The Hispanic Republicans of Texas had an office a few miles east of Westlake High School in northwest Austin, where the Texas Hill Country takes its shape heading west. The Edwards Escarpment is the proper, scientific label for the rugged limestone hills blanketed with Ashe Juniper and Live Oak trees. Elena Garcia could look out her window westerly through a beautiful neighborhood whose greenbelts tricked the human eye by giving the illusion of wilderness to the vast rooftops tucked within the Live Oak canopy. Elena often reflected on the stark contrast it painted to her childhood street. The news today, however, brought her immense pride. The unraveling of a corrupt gang was underway. A gang that ravaged young Hispanic girls. Maybe now the twenty-first century trail of tears would be examined more honestly and openly. She could only hope.

Along the Guadalupe River outside in back, Michael Darst watched from his favorite easy chair as the entire country suddenly came to grips with a scandal that dared to eclipse the recent political assassination attempt. A sense of relief overwhelmed Michael. He slowly rose from his chair and walked to the window facing the river. He missed Sue and wished she was there to share the news. Nevertheless, Michael felt that he could now take a deep breath and exhale it, all of it, finally.

In Houston, John Milton leaned back in his desk chair to take in the news, flipping from channel to channel as he talked by phone with the lieutenant governor.

Two days after the news broke, the Texas lieutenant governor and state attorney general were shown together at a news conference, where the lieutenant governor called for a special session of the state legislature and the attorney general declared that articles of impeachment were being drawn against Governor Harper, and he issued a demand that an emergency measure be drawn and circulated to provide for a voter referendum on independence from the United States.

"This country, with its institutions, belongs to the people who inhabit it. Whenever they shall grow weary of the existing government, they can exercise their constitutional right of amending it, or exercise their revolutionary right to overthrow it."

- Abraham Lincoln

The End

End of Part One

Coming soon: *TEXIT - Lone Star Rising, The gripping sequel*

Made in the USA
Monee, IL
04 November 2026

67378715R00167